THE REIGN *of* IDEOLOGY

THE REIGN *of* IDEOLOGY

Eugene Goodheart

COLUMBIA UNIVERSITY PRESS • NEW YORK

Columbia University Press
Publishers Since 1893
New York   Chichester, West Sussex
Copyright © 1997 Columbia University Press
All rights reserved

Library of Congress Cataloging-in-Publication Data
Goodheart, Eugene.
    The reign of ideology / Eugene Goodheart.
        p.   cm.
    Includes bibliographical references and index.
    ISBN 0–231–10622–X. — ISBN 0–231–10623–8 (pbk.)
    1. Criticism. 2. Ideology. 3. United States—Intellectual life—20th century.   I. Title.
    PN81.G636 1996
        801'.95—dc20   96–8330
                                                                                 CIP

Casebound editions of Columbia University Press books are printed on permanent and
durable acid-free paper.
Printed in the United States of America
c 10 9 8 7 6 5 4 3 2 1
p 10 9 8 7 6 5 4 3 2 1

FOR JOAN AGAIN

CONTENTS

ACKNOWLEDGMENTS

Robert Alter and Morris Dickstein deserve special thanks for the indispensable advice they gave me in shaping the book. I owe a special debt of gratitude to Morris Dickstein, upon whose judgment and support I have come to depend over the years. I am grateful to my good friend and faithful reader, Daniel Aaron, for his suggestions and encouragement. I have also benefited from the comments of Sacvan Bercovitch, Michael T. Gilmore, Alvin Kibel, and Robert Nozick. As always, my wife Joan Bamberger was my conscience in matters of style. Anne Lawrence deciphered my handwriting, found and corrected errors with her keen editorial eye, and produced a finely composed typescript. She was a model of competence and genial patience.

Versions of chapters have appeared in periodicals: "From Culture to Ideology," in *Partisan Review* 2 (1994), "The Postmodern Liberalism of Richard Rorty," in *Partisan Review* 2 (1996), "Arnold, Critic of Ideology," in *New Literary History* (Spring 1994), "The Abandoned Legacy of the New York Intellectuals," in *American Jewish History* (Spring 1991), "Ideology and Ethical Criticism" as review of Wayne Booth's *The Company We Keep: An Ethics of Fiction* in *London Review of Books* 11, no. 6 (March 16, 1989), "Freud on Trial," in *Dissent* (Spring 1995), and "The Passion of Reason: Reflections on Primo Levi and Jean Amery," in *Dissent* (Fall 1994). "Kenneth Burke Revisited" was first published in a slightly different version in *The Sewanee Review* cii, no. 3 (Summer 1994). The introduction and chapter 1 contain passages from "PC or Not PC," in *Partisan Review* 4 (1993) and "The Fallacy of Constructivism," in *CLIO* (Spring 1995), respectively.

THE REIGN *of* IDEOLOGY

Introduction

"The principle of ideological interpretations of cultural and intellectual life is to deny the autonomy of mind and the existence of universal truths."[1] Hans Barth's statement is an accusation and, when it was made in the 1950s, it was expected to arouse a sympathetic response in the reader. The current dominant view in the academy is that "autonomy of mind" and "universal truths" are harmful illusions that need to be dispelled. To autonomy and universality we may add other terms that have become suspect: reason, transcendence, aesthetic value. Ideological interpretation, as I understand it, has a wider reference than what is normally understood by ideological criticism. It includes the work of critics who believe that the term has outlived its usefulness and who prefer terms like *episteme* or *rhetoric*—that is, criticism that subscribes to a hermeneutics of suspicion. Even among those who declare themselves to be ideology critics quarrels abound about the meaning of the term. I have no desire to adjudicate these quarrels. My concern is with a certain attitude or range of attitudes toward texts and institutions that has become endemic in the academy. Whatever its range of possible meanings might be (and the word has a protean history), the term *ideology* as used in current academic practice describes the ways in which texts and institutions conceal or rationalize motives of domination. Its principal current meaning can be abbreviated as "false consciousness."[2] It is the text, whatever form it takes in cultural and intellectual life, that exhibits false consciousness; it is the ideology critic who discovers the truth that the text conceals.

The current varieties of criticism share a mistrust of the text's explicit claims. If, for example, the text affirms a set of ideas, the critic will try to elicit the underlying motives that may compromise or contradict these ideas. Although Michel Foucault is not an ideology critic, his own discourse resembles ideological interpretation in its attention to the silences and gaps in discourse. What often interests Foucault is what is unsaid rather than what is said—for instance, the disciplinary rather than the luminous power of Enlightenment reason. A recent critic who favors ideological criticism notes that in practice much "rhetorical analysis [which does not think of itself as ideological] looks suspiciously like critiques of ideology, especially insofar as it remains interested in the power over representation of certain social groups."[3] I don't mean to suggest that rhetorical analysis always exposes texts so as to show how it conceals motives of domination. Rhetorical analysis may illuminate and appreciate the value of a text. Kenneth Burke's criticism is exemplary in this respect. Nowadays, however, criticism generally tends to display the unmasking critic's superiority. Terry Eagleton, who writes from a Marxist perspective, represents a generally held view that extends beyond Marxism.

> Criticism is not a passage from text to reader. Its task is not to redouble the text's self-understanding, to collude with its object in a con-

spiracy of eloquence. Its task is to show the text as it cannot know itself, to manifest those conditions of its making (inscribed in its very letter) about which it is necessarily silent. It is not just that the text knows some things and not others; it is rather that its very self-knowledge is the construction of self-oblivion. To achieve such a showing, criticism must break with its ideological pre-history, situating itself outside the space of the text on the alternative terrain of scientific knowledge.[4]

Unmasking critics need not subscribe to Eagleton's opposition between ideology and science (and most contemporary hermeneuticists of suspicion do not) to share the spirit of mistrust of "the text's self-understanding" expressed by Eagleton. The mark of the critic as ideologue is this generic assumption. It is one thing to say that texts may conceal, distort, and misunderstand; it is quite another to generalize this view to all texts and to the cultural life in general. For one thing, it leaves the critic vulnerable to the same charge. Eagleton believes, unpersuasively, that he has escaped the charge by declaring his terrain to be scientific.

Since Eagleton's distinction between ideology and science owes a great deal to Louis Althusser, the French structuralist Marxist, I should note that Althusser explicitly distinguishes ideology from false consciousness. Ideology, according to Althusser, represents "the attitudes, predilections and dispositions" of a group, "its practice and lived experience," which cannot be construed as either true or false. It is not "a contingent excrescence of History; it is a structure essential to the historical life of societies."[5] Such a view enables Althusser to distinguish between the repressive ideology of the ruling class and an ideology that becomes an instrument of deliberate revolutionary action. What makes it an historical necessity is that it provides the action that science cannot provide. But we should not be deceived into thinking that Althusser has extricated ideology from the grip of false consciousness. "An ideology (in the strict sense of the term—the sense in which Marxism is not itself an ideology) can be regarded as characterized . . . by the fact that *its own problematic is not conscious of itself*."[6] This can mean either that it is mystified in its understanding of the world or that it naively lives the truth. But since ideology is indifferent to the distinction between truth and falsity, it is hard to see how ideology of whatever persuasion can avoid the perils of false consciousness. An ideology without "false consciousness" is in principle possible, but in practice very difficult to achieve.

Ideology critics write from their own ideological position without subjecting it to self-critical reflection, as if its intellectual and moral superiority were self-evident. Uninterested in how the text understands itself, they have no compunctions about aggressively translating what the text believes it is saying into a language that serves their own agenda.[7] That language is one of resistance to the destructive legacy of imperialism, racism, patriarchy, and economic oppression. they affirm the *identities* of particular disenfranchised groups against imperializing tendencies to repress them. "Difference" as a marker of identity becomes sacrosanct. Blacks are seen as radically different from whites, women from men, the colonizer from the colonized, the homosexual from the heterosexual. Difficulties, however, arise in deciding what constitutes the difference. There are differences among those who subscribe to the prevailing discourse about the identity of any particular disenfranchised group. But the differences within the disenfranchised group may give way to a coercive tendency to turn difference into a prescription for a particular way of thinking, as when Derrick Bell remarks that "the ends of diversity are not served by people who look black and think white."[8] One might respond that the ends of diversity are not served by a conception that reduces and homogenizes identity into something called "black thinking." This reductive habit is an essential feature of ideology critique.

It is ironic that for all the talk about difference, real differences are often not tolerated in cultural debate. Intolerance takes the form of exclusion from the prevailing discourse. In recent years dialogue under the sponsorship of the Soviet literary theorist Mikhail Bakhtin has been fetishized in theoretical discussion, but academic practice has confined the territory of dialogue to the politically like-minded, so that the differences that have been played out have been small and esoteric. No genuine dialogue has taken place, for instance, between radicals and conservatives, between radicals and liberals or between liberals and conservatives. Appropriately, the metaphor for exchange between left and right has been "war," as in the phrase "the culture wars." New Historicists may quarrel with Marxists over the importance of class as an explanatory category, Marxists with Foucauldians, and so forth, but the prevailing discourse excludes persons of conservative or even liberal persuasion who do not view all the evils of the modern world as springing from Western imperialism and who are concerned to discover commonalities among people rather than differences.

Exclusion means that these views are ignored or treated with contempt as reactionary. To be excluded means not to be part of the discussion; it may mean not to be taken seriously for a grant or a job. But one may object that all discourse entails exclusions, so why should the currently prevailing discourse incur the charge of censoriousness? A prominent exponent of the prevailing discourse reminded me that there was a time when literary critics were rebuked if they sought to determine an author's intention, or if they promiscuously consulted their feelings in reading texts. The intentional and affective fallacies entered into "the speech codes" of the New Criticism.

The analogy between then and now is false. It was always possible then to contest the intentional or affective fallacy without being made to feel that one was arguing a view that was politically or morally disgraceful. What distinguishes the present situation is the way in which differences have been politicized and transformed into ideological encounters. Every community, no matter how generous and inclusive its accommodation of political differences, has a view of what is outside the pale. An intolerance of Holocaust revisionism, for instance, is not itself a sign of general intellectual intolerance. We sense intolerance when what is viewed as outside the pale colonizes more and more the territory of possible differences.

A major casualty of ideological intolerance has been the academic experience of literature. There is the question of aesthetic value. Since the aesthetic category is under suspicion and value itself is regarded as insecure and contingent, critics who had derived their confidence from a knowledge of literary tradition, taste, experience, and intellectual capacity are now told that their judgments are without capacity. The field of judgment is then left to politics, or to a certain kind of politics that determines what stays in, what stays out, what goes in, what goes out. If the idea of a canon does not disappear, it must learn to endure constant revision. The revision of the canon does not necessarily entail exclusion of its inhabitants: it may mean a new understanding motivated by suspicion of concealed motives of domination and by a passion for demystification. It discovers sexism in Rabelais, colonialism in Shakespeare, complicity with patriarchy in Jane Austen. The new ideological focus tends to produce a code of political correctness once one has decided to take this route. The temptation is strong to judge texts according to contemporary standards of decency. Such criticism freezes all pleasure in the playfulness, irreverence, and irresponsibility of the imagination. It is blind and deaf to the possible truth in ideas and attitudes that do not satisfy contemporary standards. Critics who take this route may find pleasure in Shakespeare diminished when discovering a colonialist motive in the plays. Their reading of *Heart of Darkness* may be an indictment of its putative imperialist imagination and a prelude to a decision that the text be eliminated from the canon. (*Heart of Darkness* remains a central text for its hostile critics, however, as a powerful negative example for ideological instruction.) Jane Austen's marriage plots are transformed from vehicles of delight, and even fulfillment, to structures for the oppression of women.

The object of criticism may extend beyond particular novels to the genre itself. Edward Said, for example, conceives of the modern novel and imperialism as being inextricably linked together, not simply in the novel's content but in its form as well. "I am not trying to say that the novel—or the culture in the broad sense— 'caused' imperialism, but that the novel, as a cultural artifact of bourgeois society, and imperialism are unthinkable without each other. Of all the major literary forms, the novel is the most recent, its emergence the most datable, its occurrence the most Western, its normative pattern of social authority the most structured; imperialism and the novel fortified each other to such a degree that it is impossible, I would argue, to read one without in some way dealing with the other."[9]

To make his case, Said adduces examples in which the imperialism is formal rather than thematic, as in the encyclopedic attempt of *Ulysses* to encompass all reality. "When you can no longer assume that Britannia will rule the waves together, you have to reconceive reality as something that can be held together by you the artist, in history rather than geography. Spatiality becomes, crucially, the characteristic of an aesthetic rather than of political domination, as more and more regions—from India to Africa to the Caribbean— challenge the classical empires and their cultures."[10] Said has caught hold of a truth about Joyce's ambition to encompass all reality but, in his metaphorical application of imperialism to *Ulysses* and other novels with comparable ambition, he illicitly insinuates sinister associations of political and economic imperialism. How does one reconcile this view with the voices in *Ulysses* that speak out for Ireland against the English colonizer or the voice of the Jew against bigotry and persecution? Said is a revealing case, because he is a critic of extraordinary intelligence and erudition with Erich Auerbachean high canonical tastes whose theoretical commitments run counter to those tastes.[11] One sometimes has the feeling in reading him that his theory compels him to demystify in spite of himself. Even in writing about the "imperial" ambition of *Ulysses* and other modernist works, one senses a lingering admiration for it as a reflection of the aesthetic power of the work. But among critics who follow Said, the tension usually gets resolved in favor of a wholehearted demystification of the imperialist adversary.[12]

Even more than imperialism, marriage has come to be identified as a repressive structure intrinsic to the very form of the novel. By imposing a normative view of marriage, so the argument goes, the novel effectively marginalizes sexual deviance. Writing from this perspective, critics often up the ante and, in language drawn from Foucault, speak of the disciplinary and policing function of the novel.[13] A valuable insight into the perils of "privileging" the marriage plot is grossly inflated into a view of marriage as an institution of oppression with the novel as its chief cultural weapon.

Thus the critic does not read a novel by Jane Austen to appreciate the "argument" it is making for a happy marriage. Suspicious of the institution as a site of oppression, he or she is rather bent on uncovering relationships of power between men and women, that is, of domination and subordination that the novel either conceals or discloses without its fully acknowledging it. A critic without ideological blinders, sympathetic to the author's intentions, might propose the following readings of Austen's novels. Darcy's masculine authority in *Pride and Prejudice* is a benign presence in the world of the novel. When it threatens to be oppressive, it is checked by Elizabeth's satiric intelligence. Knightley's mentorship of Emma (in the novel of that name) is similarly benign; the guarantee against its becoming oppressive lies in Emma's irrepressible willfulness and fancy.[14] The ideological objection to such a reading is that it would seem to endorse the patriarchal structure of marriage. The specter of patriarchal domination simply blocks thought about the value of Knightley's mentorship and Darcy's aristocratic authority. Moreover, the relatively benign marriages of Elizabeth and Darcy and Emma and Knightley (however one construes their moral value) are seen as idealized falsifications of historical reality, since power in actual marriages of the time was unequally distributed between men and women to the overwhelming advantage of men. Austen imagined something approaching equality between Darcy and Elizabeth, an equality that rarely, if ever, existed in Austen's time.

One can agree that the marriage of Elizabeth and Darcy and that of Emma and Knightley are imaginative constructions without conceding the argument to the ideology critics. For their unwarranted assumption is that the novel is a realistic historical document, not a literary or narrative "argument" for a particular view of society. It asks not to be judged against the historical facts of marriage in Austen's time, but according to a moral ideal of what constitutes a rational and loving marriage relationship. The motive of the ideological attack upon the marriage plot is the animus of the critic against the institution of marriage. The critic in effect rewrites the novel to reflect his or her animus. By refusing to allow the argument of the novel to make its claim on the reader, the ideology critic silences what the novel may teach us about marriage at a time like our own in which the power relations have changed dramatically from what they were in Austen's time. The effect of ideological reduction is to deprive the novel of its voice in the contemporary scene. The view that gender roles as conceived in works of the past have nothing to contribute to a conception of humane civilization is so strong among some practitioners of feminist ideology critique that we have difficulty trying to recapture, for example, what Jane Austen understood as ideal relations between men and women.

A novelist's rewriting of another's novel is no crime. The literary tradition is filled with instances of writers who have rewritten the works of predecessors. George Eliot's *Adam Bede* rewrites Hawthorne's *The Scarlet Letter*, Saul Bellow's *Adventures of Augie March* rewrites Twain's *Adventures of Huckleberry Finn*, and D. H. Lawrence reconceives the endings of Hardy's novels in his *Study of Thomas Hardy* and in his own novels. Rewriting is the form originality takes within the tradition. But, I believe, a distinction is to be made between rewriting as an imaginative act and rewriting as a critical act. For the imaginative writer, the work of the predecessor is a provocation, a source of inspiration for the telling of his or her story. It is not meant to censor or substitute for the predecessor's work. By contrast, the critical act is or should be an exercise in judgment with an obligation to hear and do justice to the voice in the work. If governed by the reader-centered view that the text is for all practical purposes a function of reading with no life of its own, then the rewriting of the text in effect substitutes its authority for the authority of the predecessor text. The value of the text lies in its rewritten version. The original text, the putative object of criticism, has been rendered mute.

I can illustrate the distinction between an aggressive creative response and a repressive critical one in the work of Chinua Achebe. Achebe is within his creative rights, so to speak, in declaring himself against the "latter-day colonialist critic—[who] sees the African writer as a somewhat unfinished European who with patient guidance will grow up one day and write like every other European, but meanwhile must be humble, must learn all he can, and, while at it, give due credit to his teachers in the form of either direct praise or even better, since praise sometimes becomes embarrassing, manifest self-contempt." Achebe's reply to what he experiences as a kind of cultural intimidation by Africa's former European masters is to affirm a creative future for African writers, independent of Europe.

> Most African writers write out of an African experience and out of commitment to an African destiny. For them that destiny does not include a future European identity for which the present is but an apprenticeship. And let no one be fooled by the fact that we write in English, for we intend to do unheard of things with it."[15]

Achebe here is claiming creative originality for the future, and not for the present. For the present, Achebe understands the necessity of "a European apprenticeship" and of the unavoidability of writing in English. We may wonder about his prescience and confidence in doing or hearing unheard of things. But confidence-bolstering manifestos legitimately belong to the literary tradition. When, however, Achebe performs as a literary critic in his reading of *Heart of Darkness* and transforms it into a racist and imperialist tale, he means to render it mute (i.e., banish it from the canon). It is not enough that he wants to put himself and other African writers in competition with Conrad. He wants to preempt the field and eliminate him from the competition altogether.

Said agrees with Achebe that *Heart of Darkness* is the work of an imperial imagination, but he wants it in the curriculum, if only to elicit from it the sense of devastation, waste, and barbaric cruelty of the imperial adventure. "[Conrad] permits his later readers to imagine something other than Africa carved up into dozens of European colonies, even if, for his own part, he had little notion of what that Africa might be."[16] But having conceded Conrad's value as Achebe does not, Said cannot resist ideological moralizing: "As a creature of his time, Conrad could not grant the natives their freedom, despite his severe critique of the imperialism that enslaved him." On this view, Conrad becomes a prime minister of an imperial nation with the power to emancipate colonized peoples. Even if Conrad wanted to grant freedom, it is not clear how this could be accommodated within a work of art.

Resistance to ideological reduction has its own perils. In their defensiveness, critics of ideological interpretation may fail to hear what is of value in the interpretations, reproducing in their own formulations the intolerance and resentments they find in their adversaries. One feels in much of the neoconservative critique of the demystifiers of our cultural life a counter ideology, which it simply refuses to acknowledge. But even those who do not subscribe to a particular political ideology and who wish to protect literature and culture from servility to any and all causes may defeat their own purposes by conceiving the conflict in Manichean terms. What is lost in the process is the zone of complexity and value that is the territory of imaginative fiction and serious thought. Harold Bloom's recent jeremiad against the demystifiers is excessive in its desire to secure the aesthetic against contamination by political, ethical and historical approaches.[17] There is no reason that one cannot simultaneously cultivate an historical awareness and an aesthetic appreciation of a work. Indeed, without an historical sense of one's position as a critic, one might fail in one's aesthetic response, as Matthew Arnold did when he found Chaucer to be insufficiently serious. In Bloom's own practice, it should be remarked, the aesthetic is hardly a thing in itself: it is a discipline of psychology.

The alternative to ideology critique or historicist interpretation or reductive rhetorical analysis is not a purely aesthetic criticism, as if such a thing ever existed. Aesthetic criticism has been shown to contain moral and political interests, although it is not exhausted by those interests. The alternative, it seems to me, is a nonreductionist cultural criticism responsive to the "text," whether literary, historical, or institutional. It asks the question Coleridge asked of the texts that engaged his attention—What does it mean?— assuming by the question that truth or value may be contained in that meaning. "Politics," "morality," "history," "ideology" remain within the purview of criticism, as I understand it. What should be resisted is the tendency for any term to become a ruling term that excludes or represses the other terms. One result would be a return from exile of banished words such as *autonomy, transcendence, truth* (not enclosed in quotation marks), and *universalism,* and their reenfranchisement in serious cultural debate.

The cultural critic is committed to an ideal of social or cultural vitality. Since society and culture are the sites of conflicting energies, ideas, and tendencies, the problem always is to guard against excess in one direction or another. The mind of the cultural critic (as distinguished from the ideology critic) is not in thrall to a particular idea or perspective. Cultural critics cannot, of course, avoid inhabiting a perspective, but they are not content to rest within it. Aware of its limitations, these critics try to enlarge it by responding to, or entering, other perspectives. The essays that follow have in common, among other things, a vigilance about reductive or appropriative statements in the service of one or another ideological agenda. They reject the fashionable idea that there is nothing but ideology and another fashionable idea that the perspectival character of our knowing makes universals unthinkable. In other words, they are impressed by Enlightenment arguments about the possibility of rational discourse and religious or metaphysical arguments about the possibility of transcendence. Above all, I would hope that the spirit of these essays exemplifies, however imperfectly, the virtues they are trying to foster.

CHAPTER ONE

From Culture to Ideology

I harbor a suspicion that *postmodern* is a vacuous term, but I find myself using it to characterize the contemporary scene. In describing the status of culture in the postmodern phase, I would identify it with a word to which in spirit it was opposed in the nineteenth and early twentieth centuries: *ideology.* Some anthropologists and literary critics speak of the ideology of a people, meaning what others would characterize as its culture. According to Terry Eagleton, "Ideology, or culture, [denotes] the whole complex of signifying practices and symbolic processes in a particular society; it . . . allude[s] to the way individuals 'lived' their social practices, rather than to those practices themselves, which would be the preserve of politics, economics, kinship theory, and so on." He goes on to distinguish this view, which he values, from the more limited "sense of 'culture,' which confines itself to artistic and intellectual work of agreed value etcetera."[1]

Eagleton is availing himself of a familiar anthropological conception, shared, for instance, by T. S. Eliot, who in contrast to Matthew Arnold, envisaged culture as inclusive of "all the characteristic activities of a people: Derby Day, Henley Regatta, Cowes, the twelfth of August, a cup final, the dog races, the pin table, the dart board, Wensleydale cheese, boiled cabbage cut into sections, beetroot in vinegar, nineteenth-century Gothic churches and the music of Elgar."[2] Eagleton's Marxizing contribution is to place this valuable extension of culture under the aegis of ideology with its inevitable associations with false consciousness.[3] To be sure, ideology has other meanings as well, but the strong meaning of false consciousness persists, and it has a deflationary effect on the idea of culture, not to be found in Eliot, or for that matter in Eagleton's mentor Raymond Williams.

The convergence of culture and ideology represents a reversal of perspective. During the nineteenth century, culture came into being as an optic through which the mechanical degradation of human life was seen and judged. In arrogating to itself the spiritual authority of failing religious dogma, culture (I am speaking of it as a character or personality) claimed or aimed to be disinterested, free of the contaminations of the social and political practices it scrutinized. It drew its inspiration from idealizations of the preindustrial past: the medievalism of Carlyle, Ruskin, George Eliot, and Morris; the Hellenism of Arnold and the Renaissance of Pater. Culture represented a continuity with the past that modern life seemed determined to destroy. The advocates of culture understood that the past was not simply to be identified with their figuring of it. They were concerned to disengage values that were at best imperfectly realized in the past in order to remake the present.[4]

The tables have been turned. Modern thought (Marx, Nietzsche, and Freud come to mind) tends to suspect all idealistic critiques of society. It aims to demystify pretensions to transcendence and to subvert distinctions between culture and society, art and politics that imply the possibility of transcendence. Social and political categories have become totalizing. What has virtually disappeared is the sense of culture or art as a force resistant to ideology. Ideology critique exposes the ways in which cultural expressions conceal class and by extension race and gender interests. It is something of an irony that this reversal of perspective in which culture comes to be seen an ideological construction has been given the name of *cultural studies*. The more appropriate name would be *ideology studies*.

In speaking of a modern tendency and in invoking such historical figures as Marx and Freud, I have illustrated my uneasiness about the postmodern as defining a period. It may be no more than the exacerbation of the modern tendencies that precede it.

The critique of ideology depends on one of the most fundamental distinctions in human thought, the distinction between appearance and reality. Rooted in common experience, it tells us not to put too much trust in appearances. Like modern science, it assumes a reality invisible to the senses. The distrust of appearances may serve a transcendental view of experience in which material reality (social, political, economic) is seen as a distorted shadow of the real. The archetypal instance of this kind of reasoning is to be found in the Socratic theory of ideal forms. Such reasoning would seem to be the reverse of ideological reduction, but it shares with ideology critique a sense of alienation from phenomenal reality.

For the ideology critic, the benign appearances of the established order in its political and cultural expressions are suspect, as they mask a pervasive reality of domination, for instance, by presenting particular interests under the aspect of objectivity or universality. Eagleton puts it bluntly. "We are generally right to suspect that appeals to see the object as it really is can be decoded as invitations to see it as our rulers do."[5] In the same spirit, John B. Thompson defines the study of ideology as the examination of "the ways in which meaning (or signification) serves to sustain relations of domination."[6] Because of their seductive aesthetic power, cultural texts may turn out to be the worst offenders. One need not assume that the text or its author engages in conscious deceit, for the text does not know itself. The raison d'être of ideology critique is to liberate the truth of the text from its mystifications.[7]

Ideology critique would seem to be at odds with antifoundationalist perspectivism (the dominant postmodern epistemology). The perspectivist resists all objective claims to truth, whereas ideology critics imply in their very activity that they possess not only an objective knowledge of self-interest and power, but also a superior moral grasp of the cultural and historical situation in which they find themselves. The difference between the ideology critic and the antifoundationalist perspectivist reveals itself in the judgment Terry Eagleton (ideology critic) passes on Stanley Fish (perspectivist).

> By ranking all of our beliefs on the same level, as forces which grip us ineluctably, Fish takes up a reactionary political stance. For the effect of this drastic homogenizing of different modes and degrees of belief, as in the case of interests, is to naturalize beliefs such as 'Women should be treated as servants' to the status of 'beliefs' like: 'Vienna is the capital of Austria.' The superficially 'radical' appeal of the case is that the latter kind of proposition is no metaphysical truth but merely an institutional interpretation; its reactionary corollary is that the former sort of belief is made to appear quite as immune to rational reflection as the claim about Vienna.[8]

As Eagleton formulates it, the criticism of ideology is a species of ethical discourse. Certain beliefs are superior to others in their objective and moral truthfulness, *pace* Eagleton's sneer at Arnoldian objectivism. The appeal to objectivity by those who are ruled is apparently not suspect. However, ideology critique and perspectivism have in common a precocious sensitivity to the partiality and self-interestedness of all points of view. The fact that ideology critics dignify their own beliefs with the language of rational and moral justification, appealing as they do to a tacit communal understanding of what is reasonable and decent (we all know that women should not be treated as servants), does not overcome the tension between their objective moral conviction and their predisposition to discover partiality and self-interest. It is odd, given the present academic climate, that Eagleton laments that "the very notion of ideology has evaporated without trace from the writings of postmodernism and poststructuralism."[9] Ideology remains a substantial presence, although one sees the possibility of the evaporation of ideology and ideology critique in a perspectivist view that successfully undermines any and all appeals to objectivity.

Insisting on the constructed "nature" of our conceptual categories, ideology critics nevertheless assume without reflection that ideology is a given. Nor do they make clear how critics exempt themselves from the determinisms of ideology and become truth tellers. Mannheim first pointed out the paradox of the ideological status of ideology critique. "If everything is ideological, then how is it possible to produce anything other than an ideological discourse on ideology?"[10] His attempt to resolve the paradox in the sociology of knowledge was admirable, but not successful. Contemporary ideology critics sometimes write as if there were no problem. Moreover, they make nothing of the fact that the concept is a recent invention with a history of unstable meaning. It is true that a concept of recent invention may prove to illuminate experience prior to its invention. The present *may* understand the past as the past does not understand itself. But if one insists on an historical perspective, as ideology critics do, the concept itself, especially one as unstable in its meanings as ideology, should not be exempt from the critical caution exercised in treating all concepts.[11] Ideology critics treat the concept as if it were a natural fact, not an invention, in effect excluding their own activity from critical scrutiny.

Ideology critique would not have its current authority if it did not express a general desire for truth and justice, as its ostensible target is the oppressor-mystifier. But should we accept the claim of ideological criticism at face value? Kenneth Burke raised the issue years ago in a discussion of demystification or unmasking. "While leading you to watch his act of destruction at one point, the 'unmasker' is always furtively building at another point and by his prestidigitation, he can forestall observation of his own moves."[12] Why should the demystifier be exempt from suspicion of the motives and implications of his own activity? Or, to put the case in the idiom of the hermeneutics of suspicion, why should suspicion itself be placed beyond scrutiny, and why should it be accepted as a necessary mark of critical sophistication?

The "reductionist [or unmasking] procedure," Hans Barth remarks, "generally assumes that any intellectual product has a double sense, one obvious and self-proclaiming, the other hidden requiring a special effort to bring it to light. Moreover, the first or self-evident sense is not regarded as the key to a true understanding of the cultural product in question."[13] Why, as a matter of principle, should we trust the hidden rather than the evident sense of an intellectual or cultural product? Why couldn't we apply the demystifying procedure to the reductionist method and, following Nietzsche, for example, expose the will to discover the hidden truth as a mask for the will to power.

The habit of ideological suspicion *when it becomes systematic and totalizing* tends to produce an insensitivity to "higher" values, an inclination to associate truth with a cynical view of motive.[14] Ideology critics feel no obligation to accept the text in its own terms. If objectivity is impossible to achieve, there is a question of whether "in its own terms" has any meaning. If they were simply projecting their own fears and anxieties in reading a text, they would be displaying paranoia. But they have raised suspicion to a theory about the world. (I hardly need to remark that perfectly sane people subscribe to the hermeneutics of suspicion.) The result is that critics dominate and transform the text to their own understanding of the truth.

Ideology critique derives from the Enlightenment, but it represents a development of its dogmatic side. Obsessed with concealment, it exposes the world to the light of reason, but its real motive is total mastery of the world. Preoccupied with power and its masks, ideology critique participates in the very discourse it apparently repudiates. We are "at a time," Fredric Jameson observes without fear of contradiction, "when we have *minimally* [emphasis added] agreed that *everything* is ideology."[15] In declaring ideology to be omnipresent, critics lay claim to a truth visible only to the discerning eye of the demystifier. They have an ambivalent relationship to mystery. They want at once to bring what is hidden into the light and to preserve the sense of mystery because the hidden truth ensures their authority. Resistance to demystified truth is regarded as a sign of the hold of mystification on the resister. Like deconstruction, ideology critique becomes an endless task. The bringing of the hidden truth to the surface does not end ideology, because it is recurrent and pervasive; more often than not, the object or subject refuses to acknowledge the demystification. Real debate or dialogue becomes impossible, because the ground of difference between demystifier and antagonist is not the problematic nature of truth, but the difference between truth and illusion. The person who claims to know the truth and is certain that others with an opposing view are the captives of illusion is a potential despot. The truth of ideology critics is not that they wish to rid the world of the concealed motive, the secret they have discovered. Their possession of the secret becomes the basis of solidarity. Ideology, even as an object of criticism, is a way of bonding in a post-Enlightenment world in which traditional communities have lost their authority. For the critic, ideology becomes the community he or she inhabits. It should not be surprising then that Fredric Jameson seems to exhibit no dismay when he declares that everything is ideology.

The connection between unmasking and the despotic or totalitarian mentality is chillingly revealed in *Hope Against Hope,* Nadezshda Mandelstam's memoir of her life in the Soviet Union.

In their struggle for ideological purity, the authorities did everything to encourage "fearless unmaskers" who "without respect for persons," showed up "survivals of the old psychology" in their colleagues. Reputations were pricked like soap bubbles, and the "unmaskers" quickly climbed the ladder of promotion. Every official who moved up the scale in those years was bound to use this method at least once—that is, "unmask" his immediate superior, as the only way of taking his place.[16]

It is not that deception did not exist. In fact, it was pervasive, but most of it was the product of the atmosphere of suspicion, indeed of paranoia, generated by the authorities. "We were brought up from childhood to believe that lies and hypocrisy are universal. I would certainly not have survived in our terrible times without lying."[17] Mandelstam speaks of the absence of kindness in the world in which she lived, and she attributes it to, among other factors, the constant "unmasking" of people, "the search for an ulterior motive behind every action."[18] How is it possible to be kind when suspicion is the order of the day? Unmasking in Mandelstam's world is particularly terrifying, because it is backed up by a police state. I don't mean to suggest that the situation in the American academy is anything like that of the Soviet Union. I mean only to elicit with the help of Nadezhda Mandelstam's witness the coerciveness, potential and actual, in the activity of systematic unmasking.

Reading a text in the less fraught world of the academy becomes an exercise in surveillance and discipline. The text is always under suspicion for motives it fails to disclose. Its declarations can never be taken or accepted on their own terms. If the text were a living person, it would experience violation. Certainly living authors may experience the violation of their texts in a critic's egoistic indifference to their intentions. Ideology critique is a species of reader-centered criticism in which the text is not viewed as the work of an author with a life of its own, but rather as the object for appropriation by the reader. Roland Barthes, who in one of his many roles performed the role of ideology critic, put the case for the reader with stunning candor.

Thus begins at the heart of the critical work the dialogue of two histories and two subjectivities, the author's and the critic's. But this dialogue is egoistically shifted toward the present: criticism is not an homage to the truth of the past or to the truth of 'others'—it is a construction of the intelligibility of our own time.[19]

In Barthes's formulation, the reader reveals himself as an exemplification of his historical moment, "the intelligibility of [his] time." The ideology critic does not in a sense make any discoveries, for he brings to a text or to a cultural situation a contemporary ideological agenda like the current post colonial agenda that says that all the evils of the modern world spring from Western colonialism and seeks confirmation of it.

II

Europe has a notable colonialist past, and it has often masked its imperialist aims under the guise of a benign universalism. Isn't therefore the legitimate business of ideology critique to uncover the reality of power beneath the moral guise? Certainly one can find many instances of an imperializing universality that requires the kind of severity that Chinua Achebe exercises in his essay "Colonialist Criticism." There he cites a discussion of African fiction by an English critic in which the critic praises a novel by an African for its universality in an act of apparent generosity.

> That it is set in Africa appears to be accidental, for, except for a few comments at the beginning, Peters' story might just as easily have taken place in the southern part of the United States, or in the southern regions of France or Italy. If a few names of characters and places were changed, one could indeed feel that this was an American novel. In short, Peters' story is universal.[20]

Achebe elicits the cultural chauvinism behind this judgment in the disarmingly candid admission of the critic: "Or am I deluding myself in considering the universal? Maybe what I really mean is that *The Second Round* is to a great degree Western and therefore scarcely African at all."[21]

Instances of this kind, however, do not warrant the conclusion that *all* universalizing discourse conceals a particular interest. As Tzvetan Todorov remarks, other ideologies, such as Christianity, relativism, racism, and nationalism, have been used to justify colonialism. There is no reason to believe that universalism is intrinsically colonialist. "La politique coloniale est prête à faire feu de tout bois."[22] [Colonialist politics makes use of whatever is at hand.]

What is at stake in the attack on universalism is the view that it is a mask for Eurocentrism and that Europe or the West is in its essence colonialist. This view has recently been scrutinized by the philosopher Leszek Kolakowski in an essay "Looking for the Barbarians: The Illusions of Cultural Universalism." He condemns the destructive aspects of the colonialist legacy of the West, but he regards the reduction of the European experience to imperialism and racism as caricature. He offers a compelling alternative vision of European identity.

We affirm our belonging to European culture by our ability to view ourselves at a distance, critically, through the eyes of others; by the fact that we value tolerance in public life and skepticism in our intellectual work, and recognize the need to confront, in both the scientific and legal spheres, as many opinions as possible; in short, by leaving the field of uncertainty open. And while we concede all this, we also maintain, tacitly or explicitly, that a culture capable of expressing these ideas in a vigorous way, defending them, and introducing them, however imperfectly, into its life, is a superior culture. If we behave fanatically, if we protect our exclusivity to the extent that we will not consider other arguments, if we are incapable of self-questioning, then we think we are behaving barbarically; consequently we must also consider barbaric the fanatics of other traditions, locked, like us, into their own exclusivity. One cannot be skeptical to the extent of failing to notice the difference between skepticism and fanaticism; that would be tantamount to being skeptical to the extent of no longer being skeptical.[23]

Kolakowski goes on to note a paradox in the values that he is affirming: that the values of openness, skepticism,and self-criticism have undermined European cultural self-confidence. He speaks of the European's "enfeebled will toward self-affirmation."[24] Indeed, it is this capacity for self-questioning that may lead to a guilt-ridden rejection of European cultural achievement as an expression of European hegemony.

I don't think it necessary for Kolakowski to insist on the superiority of Europe in its capacity for self-criticism, first, because this capacity is not universally actualized in Europe (far from it) and second, because the issue should not be the question of superiority, but rather of the value of criticism, skepticism, and openness. But Kolakowski is right to see the risks of cultural self-alienation in the willingness to reduce Europe to its colonialist aspect. His attitude toward cultural universalism is admirably ambiguous (not ambivalent). "My own claims are thus instances of inconsistent skepticism and inconsistent universalism: skepticism and universalism, in other words, of a kind that avoid . . . paradox by remaining within certain limits, beyond which the difference between themselves and barbarity becomes blurred."[25] What he wishes to see propagated are not European values and achievements per se, but those values that he believes Europe has in its best Enlightenment traditions nurtured in the interests of fostering diversity. Kolakowski's insistence on the universality of certain European cultural values does not reflect a desire for domination, but rather an *un*fanatical and *un*exclusive hospitality toward other cultures.

The preoccupation with colonialism, when it becomes a vehicle for resentment, deflects attention from the possibility of productive change. Since the past cannot be altered it makes sense to address it moralistically only if addressing it enables one to see and undo present injustice. It is unproductive, for instance, to want to correct history "through a return to an imaginary point centuries ago, before the colonial deformation set in."[26] Aijaz Ahmad offers the example of the futile fantasy of those in India who propose to reject English as one of the languages of India. The critique of colonialism should awaken the European conscience to an awareness of the human destructiveness of conquest, it should be a spur to liquidating the legacy of injustice still experienced by conquered peoples and it ought to constitute a warning against future conquest, but it cannot, and should not, undo the cultural consequences of the conquest. Colonialism is *not* the essence of modern European civilization in the sense that the Holocaust is the essence of Naziism. To argue the contrary is to assert that Europe is a nihilism. Postconquest Europe produced a civilization that contains within itself the potentiality for the negation of colonialism and for cultural diversity. What is at stake is not simply a defense of Europe, but the very values that presumably inspire the critique of colonialism. This I believe is the implicit logic of Kolakowski's affirmation of European identity.

The limit that Kolakowski imposes on skepticism is an implicit rebuke to its radical version that declares the impossibility of objective knowledge, as we are all supposed to be locked inside our perspectives. The consequence of such a view is the arrogance of solipsism or the confession of defeat that epistemological or ethical authority is impossible. The ideology critic and the radical skeptic have an affinity for each other. They share a *dogmatic* conviction in their possession of truth (in the case of the ideology critic) and the impossibility of truth (in the case of the radical skeptic).

Kolakowski's skepticism is an important ingredient in an epistemology of democracy. Although it does not preclude the possibility that a person or institution may possess truth, it resists all dogmatic claims to absolute truth. If power justifies itself in the name of truth, it should never presume to be unchallengeable. Kolakowski's limited skepticism, which allows for the possibility of truth, contrasts with a radical skepticism that lacks the intellectual or moral resources to resist raw power. Truth and moral claims that might justify power or that might argue against it dissolve in the acid of radical skepticism. Kolakowski's inconsistent universalism avoids the twin pitfalls of ideological dogmatism and radical skepticism.

Kolakowski, however, does not escape unscathed. He admits as much when he confesses to inconsistency, although he seems to do so with the confidence of a man who believes that he has disarmed his critics. The fact is that in avoiding one paradox, he becomes caught by another, the same one that Claude Levi-Strauss cannot avoid when he condemns the ethnocentric "tendency to discount and despise members of other cultures as savages and barbarians and speaks of it . . . as 'this naive attitude . . . deeply rooted in most men.'"[27] Levi-Strauss's condemnation of the tendency involves his use of *savage* as a term of judgment. "This attitude of mind, which excludes as 'savages' (or any people one may choose to regard as savages) from human kind, is precisely the attitude most strikingly characteristic of those same savages." Levi-Strauss does not enclose the second use of savages in inverted commas. And this is not an oversight, as Ernest Gellner points out, for "the liberal [universalist] is in great danger of falling into paradox: either he condemns the ethnocentrism of savages and thus his tolerance has an important limit, or he does not, and then he at least condones *their* intolerance."[28] According to Gellner, the paradox has its source in contrary motives in the Enlightenment, the rational tolerance of diversity and the universalist belief in life according to Reason and Nature.

How does universalism avoid becoming a bigotry reflecting a certain conception of reason and nature and therefore vulnerable to the charge that it is simply another ideology? Only it seems to me by substituting a version of pluralism that holds out and cherishes the possibility of communication among diverse perspectives. (I distinguish this pluralism from a fashionable relativism that assumes an incommunicability among perspectives, in effect permitting each perspective to become a law unto itself, indifferent to, if not intolerant of, other perspectives.) The pluralist rejects the idea that truth is singular, but unlike the doctrinaire relativist leaves himself open to the truths of opposing views. As Isaiah Berlin remarks, the pluralist allows for "members of one culture . . . [to] understand (what Vico called *entrare*) the values, the ideals, the forms of life of another culture or society, even those remote in time or space. They may find these values unacceptable, but if they open their minds sufficiently they can grasp how one might be a full human being, with whom one could communicate, and at the same time live in the light of values widely different from one's own, but which nevertheless one can see to be values, ends of life, by the realization of which men could be fulfilled. We are free to appreciate or to criticize the values of other cultures, but we cannot pretend not to understand them at all or to regard them simply as subjective, the products of creatures in different circumstances with different tastes from our own and which do not speak to us."[29] It would be disingenuous to identify pluralism, as Berlin understands it, with universalism. But if we keep the contrast between relativism and pluralism in mind, we can discern an affinity between pluralism and the universalist outlook.

The aim of pluralism is communication, the effort to discover common ground among differences: "how one might be a full human being, with whom one could communicate, and at the same time live in the light of values widely different from one's own." Doctrinaire relativism often exaggerates differences in order to make its point. As Bernard Williams notes,

> It is artificial to treat [differences] as if they always involved two clearly self-contained cultures. A fully individuable culture is at best a rare thing. Cultures, subcultures, fragments of cultures, constantly meet one another and exchange and modify practices and attitudes. Social practices could never come forward with a certificate saying that they belonged to a genuinely different culture, so that they were guaranteed immunity to alien judgments and reactions.[30]

Williams's topic is ethical thought, but what he has to say applies to epistemology as well. The possibility of commerce and interchange between points of view reflects the fluidity of boundaries. "The fact that people can and must react when they are confronted with another culture, and do so by applying their existing notions . . . seems to show that the ethical thought of a given culture can always stretch beyond its boundaries."[31] Such a view does not do away with boundaries altogether. Tolerance has its limits, drawing a line at the barbarism Kolakowski speaks of. But the generosity of mind implied in this conception of pluralism requires a careful reflection about what constitutes barbarism. Relativists who make difference sacrosanct have trouble entertaining the possibility of a shared humanity that transcends cultural difference. Consider the complaint of Marianna Torgovnick that the West projects its anxieties and fears onto Africa and that its construction of the primitive has little to do with the reality it is supposed to depict.

The primitive has traditionally (by a sleight of mind) been viewed as our beginnings, persisting into the present. But it suggests to us not only beginnings, but endings—desired endings, feared endings. It is no accident that the narratives collected by anthropologists like Levi-Strauss or linguists like Chenéviere often tell creations stories or stories of apocalypse. Our interest in the primitive meshes thoroughly, in ways we have only begun to understand, with our passion for clearly marked and definable beginnings and endings that will make what comes between them coherent narrations. A significant motivation for primitivism in modernism, and perhaps especially in postmodernism, is a new version of the idyllic, utopian primitive: the wish for "being physical" to be coextensive with "being spiritual"; the wish for physical, psychological and social integrity as a birthright, within familial and cultural traditions that both connect to the past and allow for a changing future; the wish for a view of human relationships as infinitely varied, stretching back into the past and able by inference to adapt to whatever series of cataclysms or boredoms may lie ahead. But we cannot capture these goals by projections onto the primitive or by any of the other routes we have taken thus far.[32]

I doubt that Torgovnick means to suggest that all the wishes that she ascribes to the Western psyche (the desire for beginnings and

endings, for integrating the spiritual and the physical), are not
shared by the native peoples. The widespread existence of creation
stories, not a Western invention, suggests an interest in beginnings
among non-Western peoples. What Torgovnik seems to imply, however, is that the West's understanding of the primitive is no more
than a projection and therefore a distortion of the primitive for its
own needs. The very positing of an Other in this manner reflects an
almost willful desire to defamiliarize a world that may be more
familiar than the ideology critics would like.

What is the source of the virtually exclusive stress on difference?
In a recent essay, Charles O. Taylor speaks of the demand for recognition as the driving force behind it.[33] If you are not recognized and
respected, you will doubt or hate yourself. The hatred may be displaced in resentment and rage. Recognition of the cultural other,
according to Taylor, involves nothing more or less than the
acknowledgment of its equality within the universe of cultures or at
least the possibility of equality. Nothing less will do. It is a mark of
Taylor's liberal generosity in making the best case for the politics of
recognition that he ignores what is often the case, that the demand
for recognition betrays a compensatory desire to dominate. As
Amelie Rorty has pointed out, Taylor's analysis avoids the question
of how cultural identity is constituted. Within a cultural or racial or
ethnic group there are conflicts as to what constitutes a particular
identity.[34] Indeed, black or Jewish or Irish or Indian identity may
itself be a heterogeneity. If it presents itself as unitary, it could be at
the expense of persons and groups within the community who have
rival conceptions and have lost out in the struggle. Hele Beji
remarks on the potential tyranny of identity politics in *Désen-
chantment National*: "cultural identity was a means of resistance
under colonial rule but became an instrument of repression after
the Europeans left."[35] A member of a disempowered group may feel
empowered by a new sense of identity but, when the group comes
to power, its elite tends to impose its conception of group identity.
The potential for tyranny is already evident during the period of
resistance in the behavior of the leadership of the movement. The

politics of recognition is not as much a solution to the problem of cultural diversity as it is a generator of new problems.

The debate about cultural diversity usually occurs within the context of a professed respect for diversity on both sides of the argument. The issue is how diversity is construed. Thus Diane Ravitch celebrates "the pluralistic nature of American culture" and "the new history . . . [which] demands an unflinching examination of racism and discrimination in our history." She accepts the "raised tempers" and "controversies" that accompany changes in historical perspectives, for we are now provided with "a more interesting and accurate account of American history." But she sets herself against "a new, particularistic multiculturalism" that "insists that no common culture is possible or desirable."[36]

Taylor has caught hold of a truth about the psychology of cultural particularism: the emphasis on difference is really a demand for equality. What he does not sufficiently explore are its confusions. Since multiculturalism eschews universal standards, all judgments about equality—or any other comparative value judgments, for that matter—are without foundation. One simply must accept the other as an equal. But such acceptance may turn out to be purely notional in which case there is no true recognition. Making discriminations, which is what we do when we make judgments, may imply a hierarchy of value in which individuals, works of art, institutions, and so forth are recognized and respected according to their places in the hierarchy. Those who hold difference sacred reject hierarchical difference as a matter of principle, the effect of which may be to deny the existence of actual differences.

The demand for recognition need not take the form it takes in the multicultural argument. We might want to distinguish existential from cultural recognition. A humane society is bound to require recognition of one's basic humanity as an ideal. Such recognition is the basis of equality, but it need not require an undiscriminating hospitality to every cultural achievement. The issue is forced when one's human dignity is identified with cultural achievement. The result is that cultural difference is illicitly substituted for cultural equality as a way of eluding *discriminating* judgment.

Taylor gives us the psychology of the demand for recognition. He does not provide us with the theory that supports the sacrosanctity of difference. For that we might turn to Talal Asad, who conceives the problem of communication and understanding in terms of power. From this perspective, no European-generated knowledge, however much it tries to be open, can be faithful to the reality of the colonialized Other, simply because of an asymmetry in power between the languages of dominant and subordinate cultures. The knowledge of a subordinate culture produced by a dominant culture is bound to be a reconstruction according to the alien categories of the dominant one. Power and its interests necessarily distort understanding. According to Talal Asad, "because the languages of Third World societies—including, of course, the societies that social anthropologists have traditionally studied—are 'weaker' in relation to Western languages (and today, especially to English) they are more likely to submit to forcible transformation in the translation process than the other way around."[37] The claim is that the mind of a dominant culture and the particular minds that constitute it are absolutely constrained by interests that disable the capacity for authentic knowledge of a subordinate culture. Such a claim renders impossible, on the one hand, discriminations among persons that inhabit any culture, and on the other, the commonalities that exist among cultures. People of the dominant or colonizing culture find themselves in a bind when undertaking a study of the subordinate colonized other. They must be vigilant beyond their powers not to allow the prejudices or ideological preconceptions of their own culture to distort the object of their study. They may even be told that distortion is unavoidable and that they best leave the study of the other to the other, the notion being that one necessarily understands an experience better from the inside than from the outside. The epistemology that supports this notion is a subjectivism that allows no place for objectivity. Objectivity assumes that one can see with clarity and understanding by standing at a distance from the object. One need only reflect on the inadequacies and failures of self-understanding that characterize most lives in order to see how vulnerable the subjectivist view is. In any case, dominant subjects find themselves in something of a bind. They must attempt to know the other, but never presume to know it, because their knowledge, given their cultural position, is unreliable. Dominant subjects wind up mistrusting their own claims about the other and suspicious, indeed guilty, about their social and cultural experiences.

Asad and others do not consider the obverse situation of the possibility or impossibility that exists for members of a subordinate culture of entering the mindset of the superior culture. For example, servants know the minds of their masters better than masters know their servants. The reason lies in the dependency of the servant on the master for survival. Indeed, so intimate do servants become with the motives and wishes of their master, that they may internalize them. If this is so, it is wrong to assert categorically the impossibility of access to other minds. The master can afford to be indifferent to the servant and to take him or her for granted. There are also circumstances in which the master, for his own well-being, needs to know the mind of the servant and finds access to it. Of course, power, conceit, and willfulness can produce in the dominant mind a distorted view of things, just as resentment and indignation in the subordinate mind can distort judgment, but the possibility of distortion hardly amounts to the impossibility of communication.

The insistence on the sui generis character of cultures, their intransitiveness, so to speak, easily turns into obscurantism. Should white Europeans pass judgment on African or Asian culture or vice versa? The answer, I should think, would depend on the quality of the judgment; to answer "absolutely no" would be to deny a priori a common humanity. What is at issue here is not whether cultures are the same or different from one another (they may, of course, be the same and different in their various aspects), but whether we can gain access to the truth of another culture.

Tzvetan Todorov offers the example of "the conquest of America." His book with that title has as its subject the conquistador mentality in its variety. Columbus is distinguished from Cortés, Cortés from Las Casas, Durán from Sahagun. Todorov contends that Columbus was incapable of seeing or understanding the other apart from the beliefs that he brought with him from Europe. "He is not concerned to understand more fully the words of those who speak to him, for he knows in advance that he will encounter Cyclopes, men with tails, and Amazons."[38] In projecting his own values onto the Indians, Columbus divinizes or demonizes them, but "he does not grant the Indians the right to have their own will . . . he judges them, in short, as living objects" (48).

By contrast, Cortés *does* have the capacity for understanding the other, despite or perhaps because of his European Christian formation. This capacity and the lack of it in Montezuma may explain in large part the Spaniard's victory in the face of the numerically superior forces of the Aztecs. Ideology here does not prevent knowledge of the other; it may even become a catalyst of knowledge: "The Jesuitical attempt to rationalize Christian religion generates . . . the separation of faith and reason, and the possibility of sustaining a non-religious discourse concerning religion" (83). The Dominican Diego Durán, who came to live in Mexico during the 1540s, is an even more impressive example of a successful "desire to know" the Indians from the inside. Although his "purpose was and is that of warning our priests of the mysteries and idolatrous practices of these people, so that they may be aware of and wakeful for some survivals of ancient heathen beliefs that might still linger," Todorov argues that "Durán's success [both as student of Aztec customs and as penetrating critic of Spanish behavior] is incontestable" (203). Durán is an example of cultural hybridization, of the capacity to be both inside and outside two cultures. Todorov carefully specifies the powerful Christian influences on Durán's life and work, but they never constitute the total explanation. He distinguishes between knowledge and compassion. You may know another in order to appreciate and cherish the life of the other (Durán), or you may also know in order to conquer and destroy (Cortés). Todorov's anti-imperialist, anticolonialist credentials are beyond dispute. As a Bulgarian exile from Soviet imperialism, he is precociously sensitive to imperialism of all kinds. As he says in the epilogue: "For Cortés, the conquest of knowledge leads to the conquest of power. I take the conquest of knowledge from his example, even if I do so in order to resist power." He considers it frivolous to "merely condemn the wicked conquistadors and regret the noble Indians" (254). Such *Manichean* oppositions (my word, not Todorov's) prevent one from acknowledging the "occasional superiority" of European culture (for instance, in its developing knowledge of the other, a necessary condition for preventing future conquests of power). The question of difference of course, is not confined to the relationship between cultures. It arises within "advanced" cultures characterized by diversity of experience and perspective.

Relativists of the radical kind tend to insist on the incommeasurability of perspectives and the inevitable miscommunication between them. Such pluralists as Kolakowski and Berlin welcome the opportunity to enter the minds of others not only to gain insight into them but to understand their own minds better, that is, both their strengths and their limitations. Berlin's liberal appreciation of the illiberal antidemocratic Joseph de Maistre reflects the pluralist's appropriation of what is valuable in a powerful and incisive, although uncongenial, mind. (The appreciation has its limits: it does not permit de Maistre's reactionary views to overwhelm the liberal position.) Kolakowski's inconsistent universalism is consonant with Berlin's liberal recognition of the genius of the reactionary de Maistre and with John Stuart Mill's appreciation of the conservative Coleridge. (Kolakowski's blanket dismissal of the barbarism of exclusion and intolerance can be criticized for its failure to specify truths and values in systems of thought that are intolerant of other systems.) Pluralism understood in this way keeps lines of communication open in the wake of the shattering of the illusions of an absolutist universalism. It thrives in inconsistency, in the incompatibility of values and principles. In the words of Isaiah Berlin, "the world in which what we see as incompatible values are not in conflict is a world altogether beyond our ken; [the] principles which are harmonized in this other world are not the principles with which, in our daily lives, we are acquainted; if they are transformed, it is into conceptions not known to us on earth. But it is on earth that we live, and it is here that we must believe and act."[39] Berlin would have it both ways. Communicate as if understanding were possible; know, however, that the utopian dream of complete harmony is both impossible and undesirable.

The task of criticism for writers for whom the Enlightenment remains a *philosophia perennis*, then, is not to transcend difference in the sense of erasing it, but to show the way different views can communicate with one another and find common ground across group lines. Such communication cannot occur without a respect for differences among *persons* within groups as well as differences between groups. (In *The Defeat of the Mind*, Alain Finkielkraut gives a persuasive account of the losses incurred by the banishment of universals, but he shows insufficient sensitivity to the problem of how difference can be accommodated to a universalist outlook.) The obstacles to genuine dialogue and communal exchange come not from our differences per se but from the exploitation of differences by a group to achieve power at the expense of other groups. Talal and others are right to point to the distorting effect of power on communication across differences. They are wrong in turning it into an argument for its impossibility. Kolakowski, who was on intimate terms with the oppressions of totalitarianism, is alert to the dehumanization that results from the view that communication between cultures is impossible because of radical insurmountable differences: "Explicitly racist doctrines as well as philosophies preaching the mutual incommunicability of cultures, and thus the impossibility of adopting a common notion of humanity, are no less antagonistic to humanity than communist-totalitarian ideologies. Their negative common ground consists exactly in the denial of being human as a universal category, applicable to each individual human being, confirmed by the inviolability, irreplaceability and unexchangeability of the person."[40]

III

The classical Enlightenment affirmed the virtue of self-criticism but did not always practice it. Its demystifying suspicion of religious ideas and of Christianity achieves in certain writers an ideological inflexibility. Kolakowski does not share the suspicion. On the contrary, he discovers a common ground between Christianity and the Enlightenment. He values Christianity not as a dogma (which fosters the fanaticism that he deplores), but as a mode of thought congenial to rationality and potentially free of obligations to despotic authority. Kolakowski sees a Christian inspiration in modern science, humanism and democracy.

Europe has groped for and appears to have found, in Christian form, the measure it needed to develop its scientific and technical abilities: to persist in her wariness towards the physical world, not to the extent of condemning it as intrinsically evil in its entirety but rather perceiving it as an adversary that should be dominated. . . . The humanism outlined in Pico della Mirandola's famous *Discourse on Human Dignity*, a humanism defined by the idea of man's incompleteness, his inevitable state of hesitation, and the insecurity caused by his freedom of decision, is perfectly compatible with Christian teaching. . . . A Christian inspiration may also be seen at the roots of the ideas upon which modern democracy was founded. Locke's God, and God of the American Declaration of Independence, were not merely rhetorical flourishes: the theory of the inalienable rights of a person was developed from the Christian idea of a person as an inexchangeable value. [41]

But it is not merely Christianity's contribution to Western rationalism that Kolakowski values. He does not share the Enlightenment's hostility to the spiritual ambition of religion. He departs from the classical Enlightenment in behalf of an expanded realism that tries to account for the full range of human need and aspiration. Undoubtedly, Kolakowski's sensitivity to religious values owes a great deal to his experience of the Marxist regime in Poland in which religious life was repressed. But his insight into the value of religious experience extends to Western societies in which religious expression is tolerated. A rationalism that excludes the religious appetite leaves out of account the vast majority of human beings. The annunciation of the death or the disappearance of God reflects the homicidal imagination of intellectuals and academics rather than cultural reality. For a great many people outside of the academy, religion plays a major part in their lives. Intellectuals of agnostic or atheistic persuasion may judge the qualities of these lives as mystified or philistine. But a quarrel with a way of life does not drive it out of existence and it may even constitute an obstacle to an understanding of how and why a way of life sustains itself. Many post-Enlightenment institutional religions in the West have become more tolerant of other religious and nonreligious attitudes than their pre-Enlightenment predecessors. Christians have learned to respect—or at least tolerate—Jews, Muslims, Buddhists, agnostics, and atheists. We may have the Enlightenment to thank for this. But in what is surely an historical irony, contemporary liberal thought that draws its inspiration from the antireligious spirit of the classical Enlightenment, reveals its own intolerance when it imagines a world without religion. Richard Rorty, for example, conceives of an ideal liberal culture that has eliminated all traces of the supernatural.

> In its ideal form, the culture of liberalism would be one which was enlightened, secular through and through. It would be one in which no trace of divinity remained, either in the form of divinized world or a divinized self. Such a culture would have no room for the notion that there are nonhuman forces to which human beings should be responsible. It would drop, or drastically reinterpret, not only the idea of holiness but those of "devotion to truth" and of "fulfillment of the deepest needs of the spirit."[42]

Rorty's version of liberalism is treated in chapter 2. I introduce him here only to distinguish Kolakowski's version of post-Enlightenment liberalism from what seems to me a less compelling, albeit more representative, one. More representative, because when American intellectuals think of religion, they may have in mind our native religious culture, which often provides the ground for a vulgar rhetoric of chauvinist patriotism and financial enrichment; or, if their perspective extends beyond the American scene, they may think of its militant proselytizing, its inquisitorial function. But for Eastern European writers such as Kolakowski and Czeslaw Milosz, who have known Caesar, Christianity has proved to be a recourse from political despotism. In its theocratic form Christianity is itself a despotism, but it may also function as a dissidence, a vehicle of freedom in an authoritarian or totalitarian society.

The turn to religion by ex-Marxists is a well-known phenomenon. How frequently it occurs I am not qualified to say. The usual explanation that it is a displacement from one type of religion to another may hold for some conversions. In Kolakowski's case, and in that of others, it misses the point. What the then-Marxist Kolakowski discovered were the mystifications in a theory devoted to demystification. In a reversal of roles, religion, the notorious opiate of the people, becomes a heuristic for unmasking the God of secular tyrannies, historical necessity. In societies in which no trace of divinity remains, Caesar has the justification of historical necessity or determinism. The "theology" of historical necessity is *historicism.*

One must be careful to distinguish between history and historicism. History is the word that represents human life in time. It is as varied in the pictures it offers of that life as the historians who create the pictures. It makes no claim to a full understanding of human life: the historical perspective is only one among many perspectives. Historians describe patterns that may or may not be replicated, but they do not, or should not, presume to make laws. The "meaning" of history for the historian is always subject to contestation; indeed, many historians avoid the question of meaning.

Historicists, on the other hand, view history as the source of an all-encompassing explanation of human life. They may pretend to be perspectivists in their tolerance of multiple viewpoints, as "multiple as the interests and prejudgments that make up the rational decisions within any given context."[43] But this perspectivism often evaporates in practice. That is, perspectivism may become, in the hands of the historicist, a stalking horse to make room for a particular historical point of view that then occupies all the space of history. The historicist begins by asserting that history is a construction, not a fact of nature, but then conveniently forgets that, in the words of Karl Popper, "it is we who select and order the facts of history" and implies that "history itself, or the history of mankind, determines, by its inherent laws, ourselves, our problems, our future, and even our point of view."[44] Historicists might not state their position in this manner, but the belief is implied when they point triumphantly to history for explanation or confirmation: that is, to their own construction, not to the thing itself. A social construction, history paradoxically acquires the inexorable force of nature or deity.

Historicists have an antiempiricist bias; they see history not as a product of observations but rather as a construction according to an idea of historical determinism.[45] Nadezshda Mandelstam describes the effect of historical determinism (Stalinist style) on the perception of real life: "The blueprints had been declared sacrosanct and it was forbidden to compare them with what was actually coming into being. Determinist theory had actually given birth to unheard of practitioners who boldly outlawed any study of real life: Why undermine the system and sow unnecessary doubt if history was in any case speeding into the appointed destination?"[46] Milosz speaks of determinist theory as a vulgarized knowledge that "characteristically gives birth to a feeling that *everything* is understandable and explained. It is like a system of bridges built over chasms. One can travel boldly ahead over these bridges, ignoring chasms. It is forbidden to look down into them but, that alas, does not alter the fact that they exist."[47] Chasms are recalcitrant facts that resist the laws of history. (Empiricism or positivism for all its theoretical naiveté has at least a respect for facts, which is needed if the distinction between truth and falsity is to be preserved.) Truth then becomes the possession of whoever constructs the theory, a potential weapon in the contest for power. The result is that power authorizes the truth.

Individual freedom becomes a problem of every version of historicism. Indeed, some versions give no place to individual freedom. Individuals are little more than the slaves of history, in Milosz's phrase. Milosz describes the familiar *historical* irony by which history as liberator becomes a tyrant. "Only the blind can fail to see the irony of the situation of human species brought upon itself when it tried to master its own fate and to eliminate accident. It bent its knee to history; and history is a cruel God."[48] Of course, it is not history that is God, but the will to power that masks itself as history. In *The Betrayal of the Intellectuals,* Julien Benda writes of "the dogma that history is obedient to scientific laws" as the preachment of "partisans of arbitrary authority." He goes on to notice that "this is quite natural, since it eliminates the two realities they most hate, that is, human liberty and the historical action of the individual."[49] A Marxist may argue that it is historical necessity that authorizes the revolutionary will to transform the world. Such a view, I believe, reverses cause and effect. The will is not the agent of necessity, necessity is the masking agent of the despotic will. The necessitarian says in effect: there are no alternatives to what I desire. To affirm the idea of freedom against historical determinism is not to deny the existence of constraining and conditioning factors in history: it is to resist the illicit substitution of the despotic will for the historical process, or more accurately, its masking by the historical process. We are sufficiently constrained in our actions not to want to be burdened by unnecessary constraints imposed by coercive authority.

And what of Milosz's and Kolakowski's Christian God? Has he not also committed cruelties, or haven't cruelties been committed by human beings in his name? The difference lies precisely in the transcendent character of God. The cruelty of the *practice* of Christianity (indeed, of religion in general) lies in its betrayal of the knowledge of the distance between man and God.

Ideological thinking entails the view that human life is a social and historical construction. Marxists speak of class, but the ingredients of social construction may include race, gender, and ethnicity, anything that generalizes the person to a group identity. The choice of group identity reflects a view of where the site of significant struggle is, for constructivist ideology, in its present use, is born out of a perception of conflict between those who dominate and those who are dominated: upper versus lower class, male versus female, white versus black. By denying or minimizing the effect of individual biology (nature is anathema in constructivist discourse) and by rejecting all ideas of personal transcendence, the social constructivist declares individuality to be an illusion generated by a variety of social factors that intersect in the making of the person. "Nothing must ever go beyond the description of man's behavior as a member of a social group."[50] If individuality is an illusion, so is the idea of individual freedom. What compensates for the absence of freedom is the power gained from membership in the group. "Membership" may be a misleading term, since it implies the possibility of choice: you can choose to be or not to be a member. On the constructivist view, you have no choice, since identity is constituted by the social group. The choice not to identify yourself with the group betrays your identity. Constructivism denies or minimizes the effect of individual will and rejects the possibility of personal transcendence.

It is by no means self-evident, as constructivists seem to think, that the person is a social construction. Note I am addressing the view that society *totally* constructs the person, not the idea with which one can hardly quarrel that the self is conditioned by social circumstance. Sociology may take as its subject the social construction of reality, but there is no justification for transforming a disciplinary perspective into a total representation of reality. It is not clear how one could demonstrate empirically the totalizing view. To hold it may be no more than an act of faith. The question is then what are the advantages of such a belief, since it is evident that constructivism reflects an ideological conviction rather than an epistemological determination. The *apparent* benefit is that it allows alternative scenarios for personal life. If society is a changing reality the person need not be permanently fixed to a particular set of roles. But the possibility of alternative futures does not itself make for liberation, since in the constructivist view the self remains trapped in a system of social determination. If there is nothing outside the determinism of social construction, what would be the criteria for judging the value of any particular social construction? It is not hard to see how easily social construction becomes a battleground between persons or groups who wish to impose their views on others. The rhetoric of social construction is that of power or empowerment. What constructivism does not provide is a plausible, noncoercive answer to the question: empowerment of whom and for what?

In valuing the social, constructivists evaporate "the natural." They enclose it in quotation marks, suggesting that the natural like the universal masks efforts on the part of dominant groups to stabilize and normalize the social structures that serve their own interests. One doesn't have to dispute the view that the natural and the universal have played roles in the history of mystification to regard the evaporation of the category of *the natural* in constructivist discourse as an intellectual misfortune. It is wise to fear the natural when it imperialistically declares a particular mode of being as universal. The natural may vary from person to person, but every person has a nature and needs a sense of it which resists reduction to the discourse of constructivism, so that he and she can judge for themselves what satisfies them and what thwarts their desires. Without a sense of your own nature, judgments of this kind are alienated to a group or to other persons who speak for the group. (Biological arguments bear the stigma of racism, but only when they refer to group characteristics. Biology, the natural condition of the individual body, is something quite different when invoked against efforts of society or of those who have power in society to control the body. If the body itself is seen as a social construction, what is the principle by which it can protest against its violation?)

My unwillingness to surrender "the universal" and "the natural" to the demystifier does not reflect insensitivity to the problems they present. I am trying to balance the terms we employ in our cultural discourse. Kolakowski is exemplary in this respect. Christianity, for example, is a check to the hubristic Enlightenment belief in reason, but it does not demystify it. What Christianity and the Enlightenment have in common is a universalism whose deficiencies as well as excesses require vigilance. Despite its deep attraction, there are satisfactions that universalism does not provide. It cannot make a culture or a society. The problem, one might say the pathos, of universality lies not in its deceptive masking of particular interests, but in its incapacity to keep its promise of solidarity. It does not, perhaps cannot provide the experience of solidarity one enjoys in groups. Universalism is an abstraction, a theory of fraternity, without the institutions, the practices, the rituals that make group loyalties. Even a universalist like Marx, for whom a fully realized humanity was the ideal, thought of solidarity in class terms (e.g., workers bound together by common experiences and actions).

As a practice, universalism is the experience of the individual, who has discovered essential humanity, the attributes he shares (but not necessarily in solidarity) with other persons. Universalists do not form parties, which incarnate the very spirit of faction; their thought and practice do not constitute an existing social or political condition as it does an unrealized future. Universalism is a promise, but not yet a culture: weak in its contention with groups, parties, factions that in their solidarity (sometimes a murderous solidarity) reflect lived experience. We see evidence of this in the ethnic, national, religious energies that have surfaced in the wake of the disintegration of empires.

The practical strength of the ideological critic is that he represents a constituency, usually the dispossessed; the weakness of the moral philosopher (a Kolakowski or a Berlin) is that he is without a constituency. Whatever social effect he wishes his discourse to have, he may find himself alone, struggling with the self-imposed necessity of being right according to his own conscience. The social temptations of ideology may be irresistible. But if solidarity is not to turn into the murder of one group by another, the effort must be made constantly to extend the boundaries of solidarity to the point where it includes all of humanity.[51]

CHAPTER TWO

The Postmodern Liberalism of Richard Rorty

I put forward the liberalism of Leszek Kolakowski because it is responsive to the epistemological and ethical challenges of postmodernism without being caught in its toils. The same cannot be said of the work of Richard Rorty, whose work stands as the most significant expression of postmodern liberalism. There are other liberal philosophers in the contemporary period, most notably John Rawls, but they do not qualify as postmodern in the ideological sense. One of the distinguishing characteristics of postmodernism is its obsession with the perspectival limits of knowledge and judgment. Perspectivists like Rorty tell us that objectivity is an illusion, that words like *transcendence, metaphysics, rationalism,* and *universalism* refer to an unattainable reality and only create anxiety in us.

These words have their provenance in the apparently antithetical discourses of religion and the Enlightenment. In the political sphere, they are susceptible to appropriation by ideologies supportive of tyranny. For perspectivists, the words that truly describe our condition are *contingent, mortal,* and *finite*—modest words that not only express what we are but also imply a respect for those who are different from us. And yet the vocabulary of universalism remains a powerful temptation even for liberals because of its association with the Enlightenment. How is the temptation and the anxiety connected with it to be overcome? Rorty's advice is that we change our vocabulary. We need to purge our language of unnecessary anxiety-inducing distinctions like the one between "rational" and "irrational" or between "subjectivism" and "objectivism" or even between "truth" and "falsity." In the wake of the verbal fallout, we will have the nonobjectivist (not the subjectivist), the nonrationalist (not the irrationalist). With the evaporation of traditional distinctions, the insoluble problems of epistemology will simply vanish. Rorty's work is in the spirit of Wittgenstein's strenuous effort to refocus thinking away from metaphysics—without Wittgenstein's strenuousness. Liberalism will at last have a language appropriate to its pluralistic ideal and its respect for the private individual.

Rorty places himself in a community of antifoundationalist philosophers (Isaiah Berlin, Bernard Williams, and Wilfred Sellars, among others) and cites them repeatedly for support, creating the impression of the self-evidency of his views. But antifoundationalism is a blanket term that may conceal significant differences—for instance, the concern of certain antifoundational philosophers to find common ground among perspectives and their belief in the possibility of finding it. The following passage from one of Rorty's colleagues, Bernard Williams, is a good example of his difference from him.

> There is a further proposition which some of these will believe (among them, I believe, Berlin): that there is no common currency

in which these gains and losses of value can be computed, that values, or at least the most basic values, are not only plural but in a real sense incommensurable. Some other people, however, sympathetic to the general drift of the argument so far, may at this point protest. To say that values necessarily conflict, and that the affirmation of some necessarily involves losses with regard to others, does not entail that they are incommensurable. The reference to *losses* does not in itself entail, on the other hand, that they are commensurable: one could register a loss in one dimension of value without comparing the amount of that loss with another dimension of value. But unless some comparison can be made, then nothing rational can be said at all about what overall outcome is to be preferred, nor about which side of a conflict is to be chosen—and that is certainly a despairing conclusion. Some overall comparisons can be made, and if they can, then to some degree, it will be said, these values must be commensurable.[1]

Unlike Rorty, Williams remains attached to the term *rational*, because he cannot imagine an alternative basis for making intelligent discriminations between possible outcomes. What would be for Williams an occasion for despair, however, is for Rorty an occasion for complacency. Even the most difficult case leaves Rorty unfazed. "This would mean giving up the idea that liberalism could be justified, and Nazi or Marxist enemies of liberalism refuted, by driving the latter up against an argumentative wall—forcing them to admit that liberal freedom has a 'moral privilege' which their own values lacked. From the point of view I have been recommending, any attempt to drive one's opponent up against the wall in this way (the way of justification) fails when the wall against which he is driven comes to be seen as one more vocabulary, one more way of describing things."[2]

I will return to the matter of Rorty's complacency and its political implications, but I want first to address "redescription," the method that he advocates for relieving our epistemological anxieties. What is not obvious is its coerciveness, its readiness to dictate the terms of liberal culture. It shows in its intolerance of metaphysical or religious views considered to be inimical to liberal culture. I have already cited this passage in the previous chapter.

> In its ideal form, the culture of liberalism would be one which was enlightened, secular, through and through. It would be one in which no trace of divinity remained, either in the form of a divinized world or a divinized self. Such a culture would have no room for the notion that there are nonhuman forces to which human beings should be responsible. It would drop, or drastically reinterpret, not only the idea of holiness but those of "devotion to truth" and "of fulfillment of the deepest needs of the spirit."[3]

Rorty, it would seem, is fulfilling the uncompleted antireligious project of the Enlightenment. Uncompleted, because it sublimated the god terms of Christianity in its own world view. It divinized world and self. We find this view in Carl Becker's *The Heavenly City of Eighteenth Century Philosophers,*[4] in which he argues that the philosophers had secularized Christian religion. By redescribing the Enlightenment, Rorty effectively rids it of all religious associations. Having given up the idea of justification by rational argument, he does not feel obliged to justify his ideal liberal society. He is the lawgiver who provides it with its authoritative definition. The heroes of Rorty's society are surprisingly the strong poet and the utopian revolutionary.[5] (One wonders how he can reconcile his exalting of the strong poet with his project of dedivinization. What does he make of strong poets who divinize the world? And what would a liberal literary criticism with antireligious motives make of *The Divine Comedy* and *Paradise Lost?* Such criticism would demystify rather than celebrate the strong poet.)

The denial of God is an inalienable right in a liberal society, and it is understandable that a liberal would try to resist god terms since they are associated with the absolute. But what a liberal society cannot permit is the suppression by whatever means of religious expression. The effect of Rorty's redescription is suppression. By ridding the language of god terms, it denies those who have a religious appetite a vehicle for expression. Rorty anticipates the objection that redescription may be experienced as a coercive act. "But most people do not want to be redescribed. They want to be taken on their own terms—taken seriously, just as they are and just as they talk. The [liberal] ironist tells them that the language they seek is up for grabs by her and her kind. There is something potentially very cruel about that claim."[6] Rorty defends himself against the charge that his conception of redescription is coercive by insisting that its aim is not the transformation of others but the moral autonomy of the redescriber.

> It is only when a Romantic intellectual begins to want his private self to serve as a model for other human beings that his politics tends to become antiliberal. When he begins to think that other human beings have a moral duty to achieve the same inner autonomy as he himself has achieved, then he begins to think about political and social changes which will help them do so. Then he may begin to think that he has a moral duty to bring about these changes, whether his fellow citizens want them or not.[7]

Rorty provides the example of Proust.

> All [Proust] wanted was to get out from under finite powers by making their finitude evident. He did not want to befriend power, nor to be in a position to empower others, but simply to free himself from the description of himself offered by the people he had met. He wanted not to be merely the person these other people thought they knew him to be, not to be frozen in the frame of a photograph shot from another person's perspective.[8]

One hardly needs to particularize this characterization of redescription in the name of Proust. It represents an effort of all thoughtful, independent minded writers (and not only writers) to extricate themselves from alien understandings of their lives and to express in their own language their self-understandings. The desire, according to Rorty, is not to communicate and persuade others of the truth of one's self-description for other lives (i.e., "not to be in a position to empower others") but to achieve the satisfaction of extricating oneself from the authority of others. This is an account of Proust's achievement that denies him the power and ambition of the strong poet to influence his readers' conceptions of themselves. But it does reveal Rorty's bias for a liberal "community" of persons content with their own private existence, largely indifferent to the public realm. It shows him as sensitive to the dangers, potential and actual, in the intellectual's will to power. Elsewhere he gives the example of *1984*, in which the inner-party intellectual O'Brien compels Winston Smith to redescribe himself in O'Brien's own terms.[9]

Rorty's sensitivity to danger, however, doesn't communicate to his practice when he imposes his own atheistic values on other human beings in his attempt to dedivinize a whole society. This is the most serious instance of coercive practice, but hardly the only one. For example, Rorty reads a passage of a poem by Philip Larkin about "the fear of dying, of extinction" and rebukes both the phrase and the sentiment behind it. Rorty tells us that there is no such thing as a fear of inexistence, but only some concrete loss. Here is the passage:

And once you have walked the length of your mind, what
You command is as clear as a lading-list
Anything else must not, for you, be thought
To exist.
And what's the profit? Only that, in time
We half-identify the blind impress
All our behavings bear, may trace it home.
But to confess,
On that green evening when our death begins,

Just what it was, is hardly satisfying.
Since it applied only to one man once,
And that man dying.

Rorty dismisses the sentiment that it is "hardly satisfying" to trace one's own distinctiveness. He says that "Larkin is affecting to despise his own vocation, on the ground that to succeed in it would merely be to have put down on paper something which applied only to one man once/And that one dying."[10] He characterizes the sentiment as an affectation not on the basis of a close reading of poem, the sort of reading a literary critic would perform in which the reader watches for tensions and listens for tone, but rather on the basis of a philosophical or theoretical prejudice derived from Harold Bloom, that it is enough to be a strong poet and that Larkin knows or should know that one does not have to find something "common to all men at all times," a meaningless universalist ambition. Rorty speaks of the passage as a reminder of the quarrel between philosophy and poetry, in which paradoxically Larkin is on the side of philosophy and Rorty of poetry. What is at stake for me in this quarrel are not the rival merits of either view, but Rorty's presumptuous claim that Larkin is affecting an attitude and cannot mean what he is saying. There is simply no evidence for this claim. One can only surmise that Rorty is engaged in the coerciveness of redescription from a need to assimilate Larkin to his own *theoretical* discourse. He is in effect prescribing how Larkin should feel about the prospect of dying. This exercise of literary criticism hardly constitutes a threat to liberal culture, but it reflects a habit of mind inconsistent with liberalism.

Rorty's defense of redescription comes down to the assertion that it is unavoidable, everybody does it. "[It] is a generic trait of the intellectual,"[11] of whatever persuasion. But it does not follow that it is his only trait or always an admirable one. In disputing the view of Charles Taylor that "somebody's own vocabulary is always the best vocabulary for understanding what he is doing, that his own explanation of what he is doing is what we want," Rorty reduces it to absurdity by offering the worst case scenario. "There are, after all, cases in which the other person's, or culture's explanation of what it's up to is so primitive, or so nutty that we brush it aside."[12] There are also instances in which self-descriptions are superior to descriptions by others. In determining what is best, we would need something like the objective standards that Rorty believes do not exist. Even if the standard is pragmatic usefulness, the question would arise: for whom is the redescription useful, for the redescriber or the described? And what would be the standards for redescribing in either case? If redescription gives autonomy to the redescriber, it may coerce the person whose views are being described. Although Rorty means to insulate the act from the public sphere (the redescription provides a private satisfaction), the fact is, as Rorty knows, that public consequences are unavoidable.

I want to be fair to Rorty. He has caught hold of a feature of intellectual life that we need to take seriously. He understands the risks of redescription and wants to obviate them by confining it to the private realm. But as his own practice shows, redescription has public and potentially coercive implications. Rorty's problem grows out of his *identification* of redescription with intellectual life. Imagine a conversation between redescribers: it would be a dialogue between the deaf, which of course is no dialogue at all. As Jürgen Habermas and other thinkers in the Enlightenment tradition have argued, intellectuals also have the capacity to listen to one another, to try to understand and learn from what the other is saying in his or her own terms, even to be converted. Intellectual life is a tension between understanding and appropriation. In Rorty's view, there is only appropriation, that is, redescription.

One of the most remarkable instances of this tension can be found in John Stuart Mill's essay on Coleridge in which the liberal Mill enters empathetically into the mind of the conservative Coleridge. Mill follows Coleridge's own procedure of asking not whether a received opinion is true (as if the critic could automatically assume that he possessed the standard of truth), but what it means. In order to discover his meaning, Mill must respect

Coleridge's own understanding of it. The pursuit of the meaning of Coleridge's text does not exclude the question of whether it is true or useful; it postpones it. Perhaps the text can contribute to a determination of its truth or use value. The effect of Mill's reading may lead us to wonder whether Mill had not undergone a conversion, so responsive is he to Coleridge's ideas. But the conclusion of the essay assures us that he remains a liberal, although, in the light of his experience of Coleridge, perhaps a reconstructed one. He expresses the hope that by "systematiz[ing] and rationaliz[ing] their own creed," conservatives will be "led to adopt one liberal opinion after another, as a part of conservatism itself."[13] Here is an example of the appropriative impulse to which Rorty would give the name redescription. For liberal views to become acceptable to conservatives, they would have to be redescribed in conservative language. But much of the essay up to the conclusion shows that it is possible for a liberal to embrace conservative views without redescribing them—in Rorty's strong sense of the word. There is no reason to suppose that a reciprocal generosity would not be possible from conservatives. It may be that the intellectual generosity exhibited by Mill is the exemplary act of a rare mind and not to be expected of entire groups. Even so, anyone advocating the liberal view would, it seems to me, want to encourage such openness and affirm it as an ideal to strive for. Such openness, however, requires a belief in empathetic understanding, which Rorty's theory lacks.

If Rorty betrays the cause of liberalism in proscribing god talk, he fails in his commitment to pragmatism in not addressing the uses of religion in contemporary society. William James, his predecessor in pragmatism, knew better when, despite his own disbelief in the absolute, he granted those who needed them the right to gain what he calls "moral holidays" in pursuing the absolute.[14] James's sense of what counts as religious experience cannot be reduced to the pursuit of the absolute. James's own religious view reflects a disbelief that "our human experience is the highest form of experience extant in the universe. I believe rather that we stand in much the same relation to the whole of the universe as our canine and feline pets do to the whole of human life. . . . Just as many of the dogs' and cats' ideals coincide with our ideals, and the dogs and cats have daily living proof of the fact, so we may well believe, on the proof that religious experience affords, that higher powers exist and are at work to save the world on ideal lines similar to our own."[15] Given its commitment to the truth of the experiences of persons, "how could pragmatism possibly deny God's existence?"[16]

Rorty's own failure to give credence to religious experience is particularly striking given his concern for what makes for solidarity among people. He finds the binding element in "common vocabularies and common hopes," not in philosophical beliefs. "The idea that liberal societies are bound together by philosophical beliefs seems to me ludicrous."[17] (Ludicrous, one surmises, because philosophical beliefs, unlike hopes and vocabularies, are abstractions and not rooted in the experiences of people.) But why stop with vocabularies and hopes and not ask the question about their genealogy? He might find the answer in their religious traditions. Even atheists might discover that the vocabularies and hopes, now secularized, can be tracked to religious sources. Rorty is prevented from pursuing the line of thought I have sketched here by his reductive view of religious experience. Religion for him is little more than "the idea of postmortem rewards." The belief in personal immortality has declined or rather been transformed "from one's hopes for paradise to one's hopes for one's grandchildren."[18] But there is more to religion than the belief in an afterlife.

In *Race Matters*, Cornel West convincingly demonstrates the need for intermediate institutions like the church in the lives of people in the inner city. He speaks in prophetic language of the great nihilistic threat to black America, "understood here not as a philosophic doctrine that there are no rational grounds for legitimate standards or authority; it is, far more, the lived experience of coping with a life of horrifying meaninglessness, hopelessness and (most important) lovelessness."[19] And he notes the value of institutions like the church in fostering "the development of character and excellence requisite for productive citizenship."[20] Behind West is the civil rights movement led by a religiously inspired leadership, protesting against the injustice of the state. Religious institutions have been known to play an important role in resisting secular tyranny.

II

I have tried to show how Rorty's redescription of liberal culture closes itself to religious thought and feelings. At the same time, Rorty's liberal ironist, the exemplary citizen of his ideal society, is characterized by a self-doubting openness that creates problems of another kind. The liberal ironist fulfills three conditions:

> (1) she has radical and continuing doubts about the final vocabulary she continually uses, because she has been impressed by other vocabularies taken as final by people or books she has encountered; (2) she realizes that arguments phrased in her present vocabulary can neither underwrite nor dissolve these doubts; (3) insofar as she philosophizes about her situation, she does not think that her vocabulary is closer to reality than others, that it is in touch with a power not herself.[21]

This is the stance of a private person who lacks the conviction necessary for action in the public sphere. Rorty's ironic tone throughout his work creates the impression of a mainly comfortable homeowner who cultivates his own garden. He is content to hunt in the morning, fish in the afternoon and write poetry in the evening. Even if he should wish to enter the public realm, his liberal ironism does not provide the necessary resources: a communicable sense of reality, objective understandings, universifiable declarations. Openness in Rorty does not have as its aim the conclusions of mutual understanding. It serves simply as a reminder of the uncertain authority of any and all assertions and vocabularies. Whereas he criticizes religion and metaphysics, Rorty avoids politics. One may speculate, however, that the reason for his avoidance is similar to the reason for his aversion to religion and metaphysics. Politics requires the decisiveness, conviction and action that the ironist cannot supply. Rorty cites admiringly a passage from Milan Kundera's reflections about the novel that apply to religion and ideology but could apply to politics as well.

[Religions and ideologies] can cope with the novel only by translating its language of relativity and ambiguity into their own apodictic and dogmatic discourse. They require that someone be right: either Anna Karenina is the victim of a narrow-minded tyrant, or Karenina is the victim of an immoral woman; either Karenina is an innocent man crushed by an unjust court, or the court represents divine justice and Karenina is guilty.[22]

The matter, as the deconstructionists say, is undecidable. In the public realm, one must decide.

If Rorty has anything to offer the public realm it is the imperative not to be cruel, a command that applies, of course, to the private realm as well. That and the word freedom, which he sets against the claim of truth. But even where cruelty is concerned, his antiuniversalist, antimetaphysical bias turns out to be an obstacle to thinking about the hard questions of when and how to diminish cruelty. Questions about the nature of cruelty are metaphysical and therefore off limits. But they may have to be addressed if we are to exercise justice. In doing harm to a murderer or a predatory nation are we being cruel? Is it possible to be cruel in order to be kind, as the poet says? Cruelty inflicts pain, but the infliction of pain is not necessarily cruel. The doctor who cauterizes a wound wants to heal, not cause pain. The patient is made to suffer one kind of pain to prevent a worse kind. I am suggesting that Rorty's well-intentioned proscription of cruelty is vacuous, because it is accompanied by another proscription of pursuing the so-called metaphysical questions about justice and right action that would enable us to determine what constitutes cruelty. Given his restrictions, it is understandable why his liberalism would have little to offer the public realm. What is harder to understand is why he would want to impose such restrictions.

Rorty's antiuniversalism is disabling because it is doctrinaire and therefore not adequately responsive to the realities of political and moral life. For instance, he contrasts himself with "the traditional, Platonic or Kantian philosopher," for whom "the possibility of *grounding* the European form of life—of showing it to be more than European, more than a contingent human project—seems the central task of philosophy. He wants to show that sinning against Socrates is sinning against our nature, not just against our community. So he sees the pragmatist as an irrationalist."[23] The distinction between community and nature serves the *philosophical* argument that Rorty is making, but is not *pragmatically* necessary. What if someone (it doesn't have to be a philosopher) interposed himself and said that to sin against Socrates is a sin against many, if not all communities. Would Rorty then resist the view that there may be a community that cuts across communities, because it smacks of universalism? Rorty complains about the irrelevance of philosophy to the problems of the world (he identifies the philosophical enterprise with the universalism of metaphysical discourse) and offers as an alternative the concrete knowledge and even wisdom of novelists and journalists. They have the advantage of observing the actual lives of people and the workings of society. Yet it is striking how often Rorty's arguments are animated by philosophical rather than pragmatic considerations.[24]

According to Rorty, each community provides the ideals necessary for condemning and acting against cruelty. But such a view avoids the hard cases like internecine conflict between communities (the situation in the former Yugoslavia, for instance) or war between nations. In such conflicts whose ideals should be followed? Is it always the case that a communal ideal will serve the cause against cruelty? Communities or societies based on the code of honor encourage rather than prevent cruelty. Rorty feels that he can afford to invoke the communal against the universalist ideal, because his Eurocentric community contains those universalist ideals that speak out against cruelty:

> It is part of the tradition of our community that the human stranger from whom all dignity has been stripped is to be taken in, to be reclothed with dignity. This Jewish and Christian element in our tradition is gratefully invoked by freeloading atheists like myself, who would like to let differences like that between the Kantian and the Hegelian remain "merely philosophical."[25]

Rorty has betrayed his theory by confessing to the pragmatic necessity of the "Jewish and Christian element," which derives its force from its universalist conception of human dignity. "Freeloading atheist" indeed: he wants the benefits of universalism without subscribing to its philosophical foundations. This allows him to have his cake and eat it, but it does not solve the problem of what should be done when communal ideals collide. On what basis, from a Rortyan perspective, can it be determined that a communal ideal is corrupt? Rorty leaves no room for passing authoritative judgment on the moral character of a community or society—even totalitarian and authoritarian societies. But then Rorty doesn't see the problem. In place of adjudication between rival views, he offers the consolation of interminable conversation. He admits that "we do not know how it would feel. We do not know whether, given such a change in tone, the conversation of Europe might not falter and die away."[26] But the thought of the disappearance of the European conversation (an odd cosmopolitan locution for a particularist like Rorty) seems to stir no anxiety in him. His antiuniversalist conception of solidarity has its roots not in liberalism, but in conservative thinking.[27]

The failure of liberals to affirm the importance of a common culture that represents common interests as liberal doctrine reflects I believe a failure of nerve that shields itself behind an epistemological quarrel about the possibility of universals. Does a liberalism aware of the epistemological difficulties of establishing grounds for objectivist claims need to take the peculiarly vulnerable form it assumes in Rorty's work? Leszek Kolakowski suggests another way. He insists on comparing and evaluating the differences between cultures and perspectives on *moral* grounds, because he knows that cultures (including his own) are capable of barbarism. He can then preach universal intolerance of barbaric acts, regardless of where they occur. In Kolakowski the challenge to universalism stops short of tolerance for barbarism and he can assert with a moral confidence that does not require support from epistemology that "a culture capable of valu[ing] tolerance in public life" and "skepticism in . . . intellectual work" is superior to cultures that don't.[28] Paradoxically, this entails intolerance of intolerance and an unwillingness to allow a radical skepticism to undermine the condition of openness. Kolakowski affirms an "inconsistent skepticism" and "an inconsistent universalism." He defends the liberal idea with vigor. By contrast, Rorty's liberalism is literally indefensible. (The hero in his liberal culture is the strong poet, who is not required to argue for his vision.) It seems not to be a matter of concern to Rorty that his liberalism is indefensible, perhaps, one might speculate, because of his remarkably complacent American feeling that it is essentially unthreatened and can take care of itself. A European like Kolakowski, knowing at first hand the reality of totalitarianism, could not possibly assume that liberal culture does not need to be defended.

The future, for Rorty, apparently holds no prospect of trouble. It allows him to conclude that it is a matter of indifference whatever people in a liberal society decide to call the truth. The following passage is notorious and is often quoted by his critics:

> It is central to the idea of a liberal society that, in respect to words as opposed to deeds, persuasion as opposed to force, anything goes. This openmindedness should not be fostered because, as Scripture teaches, truth is great and will prevail, or because as Milton suggests, truth will always win in a free and open encounter. It should be fostered for its own sake. *A liberal society is one which is content to call "true" whatever the upshot of such encounters turns out to be.*[29]

Rorty is right to dismiss the scriptural view that truth will always prevail, but it is nothing short of amazing that he is willing to accept as "true" whatever the reality might be. What if the outcome is barbarism, what are the resources in liberal culture for countering it? Perhaps Rorty believes that circumscribing "anything goes" to the realm of expression is sufficient protection against cruelty. But the very fact that he is not willing to give the unconditional license of "anything goes" to actors (as distinguished from worders) suggests that we *should not* be content to call true, "whatever the upshot turns out to be," especially if "truth" turns out to be the verbal representation of the noxious force that he wishes to proscribe.

Irony is a negative condition or attitude: it exists in a relation of doubt or quizzicality to some positive assertion "taken as final." A culture needs something more than irony to provide it with values and with the inner strength to resist barbarism. Rorty's account of our moral lives precludes not only any and all appeals to universal standards, it refuses to give credence to the appeal to "something inside" in us.

> Suppose that Socrates was wrong, that we have *not* once seen the Truth, and so will not, intuitively, recognize it when we see it again. This means that when the secret police come, when the torturers violate the innocent, there is nothing to be said to them of the form "there is something within you which you are betraying. Though you embody the practices of a totalitarian society which will endure forever, there is something beyond those practices which condemns you." . . . There is nothing deep down inside us except what we have indeed put there ourselves, no criterion that we have not created in the course of creating a practice, no standard of rationality that is not an appeal to such a criterion, no vigorous argumentation that is not obedience to our own conventions.[30]

Rorty here exemplifies the agnostic intellectual, described by the philosopher and Holocaust survivor, Jean Amery, whose morally ungrounded rationalism could lead him to accept the "morality" of the torturers in the death camps.

> The intellectual . . . who after the collapse of his initial inner resistance that what may not be, very well could be, who experienced the logic of the SS as a reality that proved itself by the hour, now took a few fateful steps further in his thinking. Were not those who were preparing to destroy him in the right, owing to the undeniable fact that they were the stronger ones?[31]

Rorty is so bent on producing an account of our moral lives that unsettles any and all appeals to general and universal standards that he is unwilling to give credence to the appeal to "something inside." He is content simply to assert that when we presume to speak from "something inside," it can only be something that we have put there ourselves. He doesn't even ask the question of why we should want to put it there. Our task as moral agents, however our agency has been constructed, should be the cultivation of the "something inside," which enables us to resist the torturer inside us and out. It is hardly enough to say that cruelty is the worst we can do. I do not mean to cast any aspersion on Rorty's personal humanity. His sentiments are nothing but humane. But as a pragmatist, Rorty seems oddly unconcerned about the consequences of his ideas.

In *The Betrayal of The Intellectuals* (1924–1927) Julien Benda cites Nietzsche's view that "every superior culture is built on cruelty" and associates it with the modern pragmatic spirit. It would be unjust to argue that cruelty is a necessary consequence of pragmatism—as it is unjust to view imperialism as a logical outcome of the universalist outlook. On the other hand, it is instructive to note a tendency in pragmatism, especially when associated with a particularist perspective, to foster conditions that can breed cruelty. The particularist who knows only the "truths" of his own community and values its ideals may find himself indifferent to the needs and claims of those outside of his community, an attitude that can lead to a cruel indifference to the suffering of others. During the French–Algerian war, Albert Camus chose the French side, because, as he said, between his mother and justice, he felt compelled to choose his mother. Camus's choice is the very opposite to the choices Montesquieu makes:

> If I knew something that was useful to me, but would hurt my family, I would evict it from my thoughts. If I knew something useful to my family, but not to my nation, I would try to forget it. If I knew something useful to my country, but harmful to Europe and to the human species, I would consider it a crime.[32]

The moral superiority of Montesquieu's declaration to that of Camus seems to me self-evident.

Rorty intuitively grasps the problem when he avails himself of the Judeo-Christian values (i.e., universalist values), because he knows that they will fortify his imperative against cruelty. What he fails to do is to admit that there is an inconsistency in his position. I've suggested in my discussion of Kolakowski that inconsistency may not be a vice, indeed may even be a virtue, when, for instance, it checks or limits a dangerous tendency in one's own view. Rorty doesn't admit the inconsistency because he doesn't wish to allow universalism into his discourse as a value.[33]

CHAPTER THREE

Matthew Arnold, Critic of Ideology

We may wish to resist the view that "everything is ideology" and yet remain in doubt about the possibility of objective and disinterested inquiry. Because of his centrality in the history of cultural criticism and literary study, Matthew Arnold continues to be a magnet for suspicions, in particular his idea of disinterestedness with which he has come to be identified. We might reconsider the idea to see what we may learn from it.

If, as we have been instructed by contemporary theory, all knowledge is interest-driven, it would seem to be an exercise in futility even to try to make a case for Arnold's call for disinterestedness. This concession, however, may be premature, for it assumes that what Arnold means by the word corresponds to how contemporary critics understand it when they declare its impossibility. Arnold himself doesn't help matters in his principled refusal to define terms. He regarded the defining of terms as a sign of metaphysics and systematic thinking, which he disliked. The word he must have felt did not require definition, because his immediate audience for the most part did not experience the epistemological difficulties that a contemporary academic audience experiences. It may have objected to Arnold's valuing of disinterested speculation at the expense of practical activity, but it would not have found the meaning of the word problematic. The phrase "to see the object as in itself it really is" has an almost ritual function in Arnold's rhetoric; it represents a source of authority rather than a view that may be contested. It does not however follow from Arnold's lack of rigor that the call for disinterestedness is either vacuous or untenable.

The charges against Arnold can be briefly summarized. He has been criticized for naiveté. Disinterestedness is impossible because self and interest cannot be disentangled. Moreover, even if disinterestedness were possible, it would be undesirable, for it would mean self-mortification. Nietzsche and William James have been invoked against the neutralization of interest. Nietzsche remarks that "to eliminate the will" would be to "castrate the intellect." And William James asserts that science advances by virtue of the very "infusion from the will and the affections."

> Science would be less advanced than she is if the passionate desires of individuals to get their faiths confirmed had been kept out of the game. . . . If you want an absolute duffer in an investigation, you must, after all, take the man who has no interest whatever in its results.[3]

Of course, if the neutralization of interest is impossible, the question then becomes what happens to interest when it is denied. One answer is that disinterestedness becomes a mask for interest and therefore a legitimate target of demystification.

My own view is that Arnold's project has been misconstrued in the criticisms that have been made of it. What I would like to argue is that disinterestedness in theory, if not always in Arnold's practice, is not a naive function. Objectivity is not a given, but rather the aim or goal of an activity. Disinterestedness, as I understand it, represents the psychological and moral condition (not to be identified with the neutralization of interest) that makes objectivity possible. The focus of my discussion is on the social rather than literary criticism.

The subject of Arnold's social criticism is bias, the distorted or diminished view of the world that characterizes parties and classes. Barbarians (the aristocracy), Philistines (the middle class) and Populace (the working class), each suffers from an excessive or defective development of its virtue. (The Aristotelian golden mean is a persistent motif in the chapter devoted to the classes in *Culture and Anarchy*.) The Barbarian's love of liberty becomes a mindless individualism, "doing as one likes," the practical energy of the Philistines an excessive love of machinery and "the bright powers of sympathy and ready powers of action" of the Populace degenerate into a proclivity for violence. Arnold does not provide us with what we now would call a social analysis of how the classes have reached this pass, though there is a strong statement in his ironic descriptions of the classes of the corruptive work of passions and interests. What distresses him about all the classes is the blindness that their various passions have caused. This is especially true for the Philistines who "give the notion of something particularly stiff-necked and perverse in the resistance to the light."[4] Of course, the very idea of criticism depends upon the possibility of overcoming bias and interest that deflects one from the light.

Objectivity, for Arnold, means clear-seeing, what the French call *lucidité*, it also implies a view of the object, i.e. of what is seen, as something whole and harmonious. The two meanings are connected, for the capacity to see or to be in the light has a transforming effect upon the world; it is productive of what Arnold likes to call perfection. Seeing is not a condition of passivity; it is accompanied by an exercise of will, by a desire to redeem self and world from their degraded condition. Arnold would not have quarreled with Nietzsche and James about the role of the will. Seeing and willing are figured in Hellenism and Hebraism. Arnold intervenes to correct what he sees as an imbalance between spontaneity of consciousness and the desire for conduct. Though he argues for correcting the balance or the imbalance in favor of spontaneity of consciousness, he leaves no doubt about what shapes and determines the cultural life of a nation. Hebraism, a figure of will, is three-quarters of life. Arnold's critics simply misread him when they claim that disinterestedness banishes the will.

But how is this self-overcoming or self-reforming accomplished? Arnold provides us with a powerful example in "The Function of Criticism at the Present Time." "Burke's return upon himself" is one of his most memorable phrases. "That is what I call living by ideas: when one side of a question has long had your earnest support, when all your feelings are engaged, when you hear around you no language but one, when your party talks this language like a steam engine and you can imagine no other—still to be able to think, still to be irresistibly carried, if so it be, by the current of thought to the other side of the question, and like Balaam to be unable to speak anything *but what the Lord has put in your mouth.*"[5] Arnold has in mind Burke's reconsideration of the inevitability and the reality of the world brought into being by the French revolution. No longer a purveyor of abstractions ("the mere designs of men"), the revolution must now command the respect even of the conservative Burke. Note, however, that Burke does not actually reach the opposite side, for his change of view occurs within the current of his original conservatism.

We might think of disinterestedness in Arnold as an asymptote, a line drawn away from bias that approaches but never reaches its opposite. The asymptote describes a movement of thought that is contained within the limits of a perspective. It is a truism that one sees and understands the world from a particular perspective at any given moment, though it is also true that one's perspective may change in the course of time. Such a view does not, however, entail the reduction of perspectivism to a doctrine of self-interest. Nor does it imply, as Stanley Fish and others suggest, that all perspectives are of equal value. Their argument is that since there are no authoritative universal or objective standards, one cannot or should not make discriminations of value among perspectives. Arnold's example suggests the contrary: that one perspective may allow for a generous intellectual act, whereas another may not. Burke makes a contrast with John Roebuck who speaks to the Sheffield cutlers in the language of "exuberant self-satisfaction."

> I look around me and ask what is the state of England? Is not property safe? Is not every man able to say what he likes? Can you not walk from one end of England to the other in perfect security? I ask you whether, the world over or in past history, there is anything like it? Nothing. I pray that our unrivalled happiness may last.[6]

The capacity to act or think generously is, of course, a function of the intellectual and moral character of the person. The implicit theory in the example of Burke is that perspective and self-interest are not necessarily coextensive—that the logic of a perspective may dictate the overcoming of self-interest or at least of a narrowly conceived self-interest.

The effort to escape from an interest-driven perspective is misrepresented by words like fixity and transcendence, words often used to characterize the ideal of Arnoldian criticism. Disinterestedness is not a fixed or transcendent site, but the very condition of culture, which Arnold describes in *Culture and Anarchy* as "not a having and a resting, but a growing and a becoming."[7] Arnold may betray his best critical self when, for instance, in "The Study of Poetry" he speaks of "the fixed laws of poetic beauty and truth," but such a moment (and there are many others) does not warrant David Bromwich's disparagement of what he calls "Arnold's pride in owning an intelligence that does not change in a life that has no epochs."[8] In distinguishing between the epoch of concentration and the epoch of expansion (in "The Function of Criticism")

Arnold certainly shows an awareness of historical life and believes himself to be living in one of its epochs. And in offering as a model for thought the *movement* from one side of an issue to the opposite side, Arnold reveals himself as an opponent of fixity. Disinterestedness presupposes the possibility of changing one's mind, if not one's intelligence, whatever *that* might mean. It assumes the possibility of escaping from and judging narrowly conceived interest-driven perspectives, but not of escaping from history.

In this respect, Arnold has a certain affinity with Marx, despite contemporary Marxist critics who demonize him. As far as I know Arnold did not use the word ideology, but no one among his contemporaries was more sensitive to the ideological character of Victorian political and social life than Arnold. Perhaps ideology is not the right word to describe Arnold's target. What he criticizes in the Barbarians and the Philistines is, strictly speaking, "structures of feeling" to use Raymond Williams' phrase. These structures function like ideologies for they determine the dispositions and conduct of the ordinary class self, though it should be noted in qualification that Williams' phrase does not have the negative valence that often attaches to Marx's conception of ideology. Like Marx, Arnold discovers the material self-interestedness that shapes the attitudes of the aristocratic and middle classes. Both Marx and Arnold produce accounts of what Marx calls false consciousness from what they necessarily claim to be an objective standpoint. What then should we make of Terry Eagleton's Marxist critique of Arnoldian objectivity? "We are generally right to suspect that appeals to see the object as it really is can be decoded as invitations to see it as our rulers do."[9] Certainly Marx asks us, indeed requires us, to see the object as it really is, when he exposes false consciousness. Objectivity itself cannot be the issue between Arnold and the ideology critics.

The real quarrel is elsewhere. Though Arnold is a severe critic of the upperclass and of the insurgent middle class, he is opposed to class conflict and revolution. Indeed, class conflict is an example of the propensity to violence that is the vice of the populace. What he wants are morally and aesthetically cultivated individuals to rise above the class system in the hope that they can reform the classes. A class system remains, and it will be enforced by a strong state that is willing to use its police power to repress lower class violence. Arnold's sensitivity to economic oppression in the passage on Wragg in "The Function of Criticism" is genuine, but so is his conservative fear of violent threats to the established order. What divides Arnold and Marx is not the issue of objectivity, but their philosophical orientations.

Arnold's antirevolutionary views are in significant part responsible for the disrepute into which he has fallen in the literary academy. In *The Social Mission of English Criticism, 1848–1932*, Chris Baldick contrasts Arnold's invoking of Joubert's cautionary maxim against violent revolution "force [the existing order of things] till right is ready" with his call for a current of true and fresh ideas as a reflection of Arnold's intellectual bad faith. "At one moment Arnold will call for fresh ideas, and at another moment ask for these ideas to go stale before they can be allowed out into the street."[10] Baldick's caricature of "force till right is ready" as an advocacy of stale ideas is a case of simply not allowing the text to speak for itself. What Arnold says in the extended passage that contains the phrase is that new political ideas should be allowed to mature and ripen before they are permitted into the practical sphere. If they are abruptly and precipitously introduced, they may produce violence and tyranny. Arnold's view is by no means self-evident truth and it is not hard to envisage answers to it. But Baldick's precipitous transformation of the idea of maturing or ripening into staleness violates rather than answers Arnold's view, because it fails to take it seriously.

We have learned a great deal in recent years about the horrors of revolution from revisionist historians like François Furet and Simon Schama for us to take seriously Arnold's use of Joubert's cautionary maxim. It is still a question to be posed to Arnold about how one would know when an idea is ready for action. "Force until right is ready" can easily turn into a rationalization for political inertia. It is by no means clear, however, that change, especially radical change, is always to be preferred to inertia. Nor is it the case that political inertia is what Arnold advocates.

Arnold has the idealist's faith in mind as an autonomous and transforming agent. For Marx and his disciple Eagleton, mind is a creature of material or class conditions. If matter determines thought, then ideology is inescapable. Ideology necessarily plays an ambiguous role in Marxist thought: as false consciousness when it refers to the ruling class and as good ideology when it refers to the interests of the revolutionary class. Arnold's idealism of culture presupposes the possibility of standing outside of ideology. Where Marx can criticize particular ideologies only from a particular ideological standpoint, Arnold in effect criticizes the ideological habit of mind per se: the prejudices and biases of all the classes, if not of the class system itself. And he can do so, because he believes that class does not totally define the self. He can then speak of a best self or of "aliens" that exist within every class, "who are mainly led, not by their class spirit, but by a general *humane* spirit, by the love of perfection."[11] Arnold does not neutralize interest; rather he tries to reconceive it in its most generous sense. Of course, words like interest and will are protean in their meanings. Interest may refer to personal interest, to class interest or to a larger collective interest to which a person might sacrifice his personal interest; it can express itself as curiosity (an interest in mathematics or history, for instance), a desire of the mind to enlarge its horizons. Disinterestedness in Arnold works to enlarge the mind.

According to David Bromwich, Arnold took over the idea of disinterestedness from the romantics, Hazlitt in particular, and impoverished it. In the romantics, disinterestedness is a form of active sympathy for others in which the self remains substantial, whereas in Arnold the self evaporates into nonentity. This view of Arnold is excessively harsh. But the connection between disinterestedness and sympathy merits attention. In the work of George Eliot, a great admirer of Arnold, disinterestedness expresses itself as sympathy in an exemplary way. Consider the following passage from *Middlemarch*.

[Dorothea] forced herself to think of [that yesterday morning] as bound up with another woman's life. . . . In her first outleap of jealous indignation and disgust, when quitting the hateful room, she had flung away all the mercy with which she had undertaken that visit. . . . But that base prompting which makes a woman more cruel to a rival than a faithless lover, could have no strength of recurrence in Dorothea when the dominant spirit of justice within her had once overcome the tumult and had once shown her the truer measure of things. All the active thought with which she had before been representing to herself the trials of Lydgate's lot, and this young marriage union which, like her own, seemed to have its hidden as well as evident troubles—all this vivid sympathetic experience returned to her now as a power: it asserted itself as acquired knowledge asserts itself and will not let us see as we saw in the day of our ignorance.[12]

The scene is Dorothea's mind, and it is a scene of intense activity. Dorothea *forces* herself, indignation and disgust *leap* out of her, she *flings* away mercy, but the spirit of justice *overcomes* the tumult in her. Her thought is *active* and the experience of sympathy *asserts* itself as acquired knowledge *asserts* itself. The verbs that represent the action of her mind are verbs that we would not customarily associate with disinterestedness. What they are intended to show is that the act of sympathy which is also a disinterested act is the result of struggle in which interests are passionately involved. When disinterestedness presents itself, we are invited to examine the passions that underlie it, not to subvert but to understand.

Eliot's conception of sympathy has an Hebraistic aspect, the will is never absent from the struggle to achieve a just view of things. But sympathy and disinterestedness do not have an exclusively Hebraistic provenance. The historical narrative of disinterestedness begins with the third Earl of Shaftesbury for whom disinterestedness emerges as a virtuous antidote to "egoism in ethics and instrumentalism in religion" and becomes an aesthetic condition. Shaftesbury describes "the virtuous man as a spectator, devoted to 'the very survey and contemplation' of beauty in manners and morals."[13] Disinterestedness entails a disregard "for possession or use" and an affirmation of the "act of perception itself." The line from disinterestedness to the modernist doctrine of impersonality is evident, but disinterestedness and impersonality should not be conflated. Even in Shaftesbury's aesthetic formulation of disinterestedness (which corresponds to Arnold's Hellenistic view) the moral consideration remains paramount. "Shaftesbury's concern is simultaneously with morals and manners, action and character."[14] By contrast, Joycean impersonality opposes the aesthetic to the moral. Words like impersonality and disinterestedness are in a sense misnomers, necessary misnomers for dramatic purposes, that represent efforts to understand the condition of selfhood in new ways.

Arnold's most powerful biases are against class and against the unsound majority (see his essay "Numbers"). The alternative to class and the majority is the alien who in combination with other aliens forms a spiritual elite. The alien has its origins in the Biblical idea of a saving remnant. This might be the place to speak of the large and important place religion occupies in Arnold's thought. But I won't speak of the religious theme except to say something about its significance for his political and social thought. Secular-minded critics tend to be dismissive of Arnold's religious interests. F. R. Leavis, for instance, wonders about Arnold's qualifications as a theologian and philosopher, and refers with sympathy to "the many who deplore Arnold's way with religion."[15] And Lionel Trilling says apropos of Arnold: "I consider it from many points of view an impropriety to try to guarantee literature by religious belief."[16] T. S. Eliot, who is not a secular-minded critic, condemns Arnold for having made a religion of culture, thereby leaving "religion to be laid waste by the anarchy of feelings."[17] What these critics fail to see is the need religion serves in Arnold's political and social imagination. He needs a recourse against totalizing political conceptions. Religious idea and sentiment provide him with energies and values beyond the round of classes and parties, so that he can judge parties and classes. Religion is the source of the ethical, the antithesis of the ideological.

Arnold's alien is the person with the moral capacity to think and act against himself, against his class interests. The historical evidence for Arnold's view of the existence of class aliens, if not of the best self (they are not necessarily equivalent) is abundant. I need only cite Marx himself, alienated from the very class, the bourgeois class, that became the demon in his theoretical system. In transcending or trying to transcend the values of his class, Marx in effect rejects the determinism of class interest, indeed of self-interest as a total explanation of the behavior of persons. Both Marx and Arnold are unwitting allies against the dominant utilitarian spirit of the insurgent middle class. The escape from determinism is an essential condition of the classless society. Yet ideological determinism rules Marxist thought. Unencumbered by determinism, Arnoldian disinterestedness aspires to a classless society, although Arnold does not imagine the disappearance of the classes.

The question of transcendence is, of course, not confined to class. Does a person have the capacity to extricate himself from the ethnic and national determinants of his existence? Alain Finkielkraut cites with approval Renan's view that "man [has] the ability to break away, to lift himself out of his context and escape his national heritage."[18] (Renan in many ways was the French Arnold.) In the same spirit, Finkielkraut refers to Goethe's conception of world literature in which "works of literature would detach themselves from the land and enter society as individuals, no longer ranked according to origin."[19] It is not that Goethe denied the fundamental and primary character of one's ethnic existence, he "refused to make a virtue out of a necessity."[20] The implication is that for Goethe ethnicity was something less than a necessity.

To declare oneself free of determinism is, of course, not necessarily to be free of it. From the perspective of the ideology critic, the conception of the alien is ideological. Self-determination is an illusion that conceals its roots in the middle class (philistine) values it purports to transcend. Isn't the alien after all "doing as he pleases," the besetting vice of middle class individualism? If he had been challenged in these terms, Arnold might have answered that the resemblance between the alien best self and "doing as one pleases" corresponds to the resemblance between a virtue and its corresponding vice. Alienation or standing alone is not an end in itself but rather a *via media* to a condition of collective responsibility embodied in the idea of the state. Such an answer may not be convincing, but neither is the finality with which the ideology critic determines the terms of the debate. If the concept of the alien is taken seriously in its own terms and therefore not subject to immediate ideological reduction, we can understand it as an expression of a view that resists the idea that everything is determined, that is, ideological. The alien is by definition irreducible and not to attempt to reduce it is to allow for real debate about the claims of ideology critique.

The discussion of the alien inevitably slides back and forth between considerations of freedom and objectivity. How, one might ask, are the autonomy of mind (a phrase of freedom, since to be autonomous is to be free to whatever degree of necessity) and the objective view of things logically connected? The answer, I believe, lies in the conditions that cause the deformations of understanding. To the extent that a mind is determined by class interests rather than by the "simple" desire to understand, its view of the world may suffer distortion. (*May* suffer distortion, because as Todorov has shown in his discussion of the conquistador mentality in *The Conquest of America* [see chapter 1], the motive of domination does not necessarily prevent objective understanding.) The autonomy of mind is not interest free, but it cannot be reduced to class interests or motives of domination.

The powerful animus against class in Arnold is offset or qualified by the view that each class has its characteristic virtue and that it can be redeemed. Arnold never attempts to resolve the ambiguity. Or one might say that the move toward classlessness is an instance of thinking against oneself. Arnold's consciousness of class, his aristocratic affections have been amply documented. Arnold spoke for himself when he quoted Gladstone: "All the world loves a peer."[21]

But as Patrick McCarthy remarks in connection with Arnold's view of the condition of Ireland, "whatever Arnold's prearistocratic proclivities were—and they were considerable—he did not hesitate when the public weal was at stake to offer a plan that struck at the root of aristocratic power and prestige."[22]

Questions arise: Does the capacity for thinking and acting against one's class or group interests necessarily entail disinterestedness or objectivity or the perfection of the best self? What is the practical effect of *alien*ation? Alienation may be the product of a disfiguring resentment which would not make for clearsightedness; it may turn out to be a lack of connection with the world that diminishes knowledge of it. How could a saving remnant transform the huge recalcitrant numbers that populate modern society, especially if the remnant does not create its own institutions? I have already noted Arnold had an abiding mistrust of institutions. The questions are hardly articulated in Arnold's writing, but however they might be answered, the facile dismissal of objectivity or disinterestedness by Eagleton and others is obtuse or disingenuous, for the fact is that Arnold has described a possibility (realized again and again in history) of the human capacity for the transcendence of narrowly conceived self-interest. It is this capacity that makes freedom and the ethical project possible. Those who like Terry Eagleton and Fredric Jameson believe that there is nothing but the determinisms of ideology have an extremely difficult time explaining where human agency and freedom come from. Since they want to change the world, they can hardly abandon a belief in agency.

Arnold betrays his argument, however, in his identification of the best self with the state. His invocation of the state precisely at the moment that he affirms the alien provides us with a counterexample to what in "The Function of Criticism" he calls living by ideas. The state, after all, reflects class and group interests: it is an organization of power. The *Daily News* asked the right question: "Make the State the organ of the common reason? . . . You may make it the organ of something or other, but how can you be certain that reason will be the quality which will be embodied in it?"[23]

Arnold's lame reply is that you will never know if you don't try. The real answer is that the alien led by a humane spirit must also be a recourse against the collective nation when it becomes coercive and unjust, as it frequently does. Arnold never even contemplates the possibility. If he had contemplated the possibility, he might have seen that the state is an expression of the political and social imagination, its other expressions being classes and parties against which he counterposes the alien.

In conceiving the state as an embodiment of reason, Arnold is a creature of his time. German philosophy, in particular the philosophy of Hegel, in effect denied the historical realities of the state in a utopic conception of it, which it then illicitly identified with the real. Louis Althusser points out that Hegelian philosophy deformed "real historical problems into philosophical problems."[24] Solutions at the philosophical level can always ignore or finesse intractable problems in historical reality. The ironic consequence is that the utopic conception becomes repressive in its denial of the reality of conflict. The utopic conception can be invoked as a justification for repressing what resists its realizations.

It is an unfortunate result of Arnold's desire to separate the world of ideas from the world of practice that he does not concern himself with the possibly pernicious practical consequences of an idea—particularly in the light of his own Burkean critique of the violence of the French revolution, which he understands as the result of the precipitous application of abstract ideas to the sphere of practice. Arnold seems totally unaware of the Burkean force of the question raised by the *Daily News*. His response is recklessly Jacobin in spirit, if not in content.

I don't think that Arnold's response is a mere lapse. His hostility to class and his celebration of class alienation has unwitting Jacobin implications. Arnold here contrasts with Burke's association of prejudice with the "collective" wisdom of the ages.

> Instead of casting away all our old prejudices, we cherish them to a
> very considerable degree, and, to take more shame to ourselves, we

cherish them because they are prejudices. . . . We are afraid to put men to live and trade each on his own private stock of reason, because we suspect that this stock in each man is small. . . . Many of our men of speculation, instead of exploding general prejudices, employ their sagacity to discover the latent wisdom that prevails in them.[25]

For Burke class is one of the sites of traditional prejudice. The class alien as a vehicle of state reason, or as a purveyor of universal values, suggests Arnold's Enlightenment affinities which his affection for Burke may obscure. Raymond Williams argues that Arnold's position on the state is that of Burke. This seems to be misleading, since, as Williams notes, "the State which for Burke was an actuality has become for Arnold an idea."[26] The difference, a decisive one, corresponds to the difference between Burke's conservatism and Arnold's liberalism. For Burke the state has proven itself: it is tried and true; for Arnold, the state needs to be reinvented according to an idea of reason. Arnold had the experience of the French revolution to know how a utopian state (even one inspired by liberalism) can become illiberal, but he shows little awareness of the problem in *Culture and Anarchy*. The result is a tension, if not a contradiction between his advocacy of an illiberal state (note not a conservative one) and his affirmation of a liberal potentially revolutionary alien.

It is not that the state is ipso facto pernicious, as libertarians would claim. The state may be a benevolent agent, for instance, in the education of its citizens, a matter of immediate and persistent concern to Arnold, whose working days were given over to the inspection of schools. In our time, the question of the role of the state has divided conservatives, who are allergic to state power and liberals, who wish to exploit it for benign purposes. In *Culture and Anarchy*, however, it is difficult to defend Arnold's advocacy of the state on liberal grounds, for he shows in that work a greater concern for law and order than for social justice, always a mark of conservatism. Even if one wishes to resist putting a reductive label on the political tendency of his thought, it is hard not to be apprehensive about the abstractness of his use of the state and his failure to think it through before celebrating it.

There is a passage toward the end of "Barbarians, Philistines, Populace," which reveals a superior understanding of the role of the state to the one that Arnold exhibits elsewhere in the chapter. He cites Ernest Renan: "A liberal believes in liberty, and liberty requires the nonintervention of the State. *But such an ideal is still a long way off from us, and the very means to remove it to an indefinite distance would be precisely the State's withdrawing its action too soon.*"[27] The state we are told here is not the best self, it is a provisional stay against anarchy in the absence of the authority of the best self. The passage from Renan has an unexpected but striking resemblance to Marx's famous prophecy of the withering away of the state after the Dictatorship of the Proletariat has done its work. There may be a caution in this resemblance: the state rarely, if ever, relinquishes its authority, for it views the withdrawal of its action as always too soon.

It should be clear from my discussion that I do not mean to immunize Arnold from ideological criticism. He offers opportunities everywhere in his work. Thus Arnold's idealization of the state is not an example of the free play of thought that disinterestedness makes possible. Nor is it clear that the positions that he takes on the reform of the marriage laws and the law of inheritance in the chapter on "Our Liberal Practitioners" are necessarily the result of the free play of thought, no matter how much he insists on it.[28] Indeed, one suspects an overmuch protesting of the matter. But failures in practice do not invalidate a principle or a theory. In any particular case, the free play of thought may have been misapplied or betrayed.

Yet I confess to some uneasiness with the idea of free play. The career of the admirable Burke, for instance, is not so much an example of free play as it is of an intellectual *necessity* (Burke, remember, rides a current of thought). He is *driven* to change his view of a particular event by the logic of his own conservatism. The revolutionary necessity that Burke describes reflects the intellectual necessity that drives this thinking. "If a great change is to be made in human affairs, the minds of men will be fitted to it; the general opinions and feelings will draw that way. Every fear, every hope will forward it; and then they who persist in opposing this mighty current in human affairs will appear rather to resist the decrees of Providence itself, than the mere designs of men. They will not be resolute and firm, but perverse and obstinate."[29] Thought is always subject to constraints; the freedom of thought takes place within constraints, which may or may not be ideological. (I would distinguish between the *necessary* logic of an idea or view which may lead to unexpected conclusions and an ideological necessity that has already formed its conclusions, which are not open to subversion or change. If Burke were an ideologue, he would not have permitted the return upon himself, or his ideological unconscious would not have permitted it.) Arnold would perhaps agree that free play is not an absolute, but his phrase has an absolute unqualified implication that requires correction.

Correction, but not repudiation. In allowing for the free play of thought, however conditioned, and for the possibility of objective seeing, the Arnoldian view provides a salutary alternative to the ideological reduction of thought to class and by extension to race and gender interests. It means that one can think through an idea to an unpredictable conclusion without regard to whether it fits into some preconceived conservative or liberal or radical agenda. Without the capacity to do so, there is no genuine intellectual life.

Ideology critics might object that "thinking against oneself" describes their own activity, when training their critical attention on their own assumptions. Certainly ideology critics are capable of performing acts of self-criticism, although characteristically critical attention is directed outward. The question then becomes: What is the nature of the self-criticism of the ideology critic? Critics will measure themselves against their master text (e.g., the Marxian text) and find themselves perhaps not living up to its requirements. A critic's understanding of the master text may differ from that of other subscribers to the text in which case interpretive quarrels arise. But the text in one form or another retains its authority. What the ideology critic cannot accept is a view of self-criticism, that is, of thinking against oneself that would unsettle the master text or that would trouble it to the extent of producing conclusions that the text could not comprehend. Burke remains within his original conservative perspective, but he allows himself to reach a conclusion that conservatism never envisaged: the acceptance of a doctrinally anticonservative system on conservative grounds.

Disinterestedness is not the property of conservatives or liberals, although it may be employed in a self-serving way by either side. Ideally, it is sufficiently free of partisan passion that it can criticize it. It is true that Arnold's targets are frequently liberal pieties, but it does not follow that disinterestedness entails conservatism. Julien Benda, who decades later in France espoused the cause of disinterestedness, was a critic of the political passions of both the left and the right. If anything, his severest criticism was directed against the chauvinism of reactionaries like Maurice Barrès and Charles Maurras.

It is an intellectual misfortune that Arnold has been adopted by neoconservatives who have embraced the partisan passion of the Republican party. There is very little evidence of the free play of intelligence in the predictable support they give to Republicans on civil rights, the market economy, gun control. Contemporary conservatism (old and neo) has closed its mind not only to truths of liberalism but also to what counted as truths in its own traditions. Nineteenth-century conservatives (e.g., Coleridge, Carlyle, and Ruskin) were fierce critics of the ruthlessness of laissez-faire economics (what we now benignly call the free market) and protoadvocates of the welfare state. Strong government was anathema to the nineteenth-century liberals, not to the conservatives, who complained that government was not strong enough to preserve law and order and to care for the poor. The term *conservative* does not really cover the views of Arnold, Ruskin and even Carlyle; their work gives the impression of an acute and anguished response to crisis, not of ideologically driven statement. Unlike conservative ideologues of the present day, the Victorian social critics were not predictable; they showed a capacity for "returning upon themselves," to recast Arnold's phrase for Burke.

Contemporary conservatives may argue in their own defense of the unfettered free market and their revulsion from the welfare system that times have changed: that the welfare state has been established and they are reacting against the failures in the system. But the social problems of market capitalism persist. What has gone out of the new conservatism is its traditional compassion. Compassion is now seen as an excuse for big government, the product of the left radical will or liberal sentimentality.

If disinterestedness is not beholden to any party, what then does it stand for? It is a mark of the ideological character of our time that the answer "truth" and "justice" would be seen as naiveté or bad faith—as if an interest-free view of truth or justice were possible. But it is precisely the wish to avoid the idea that disinterestedness is a value-free activity that requires its association with the values of truth and justice, and values that reflect interest in the most generous sense of the term. The danger of dissociating disinterestedness from values and interests is clear enough. As Zygmunt Bauman points out, the idea of "the moral neutrality of reason and the pursuing of rationality"[30] led in the case of the German professoriate to effective cooperation with the Nazis. One could continue to do the research that led to the production of weapons of destruction without resisting their employment by the authorities. Disinterestedness is not value-free or should not be. As an attitude of intellectual integrity, it should enable the making of distinctions between the moral and the immoral. It should become the voice of resistance to the employment of reason for evil purposes. I cannot therefore follow Benda when he conceives of the true intellectual as a being loftily indifferent to the political life. Benda's image of disinterestedness (unlike Arnold's) is unsustainable in times of crisis when the intellectual has to descend into the practical arena and speak out against injustice. Did Zola betray his calling as artist and intellectual in entering the fray for Dreyfus? Disinterestedness does not necessarily presuppose the disempowerment of the intellectual. To separate truth from power in order to prevent contamination may have the effect of rendering truth impotent. The task of the intellectual is not to reject the practical sphere but to exercise intelligence in the interests of truth and justice on whatever side of the political spectrum it may be found.

Genuine thinking is an activity against the grain of ideological formulas that petrify the mind. Ideology critics, ostensibly critics of ideology, are in their own commitments to an ideological agenda ideologues, for those agendas are more often than not formulaic "understandings" of reality, whether the subject is imperialism or class conflict or from another ideological standpoint Stalinism. These formulas may spring from master texts that reflect genuine, even profound thinking, a text by Marx, for instance, but the sense of complication and difficulty of the text has been lost in the mind of the ideology critic, who no longer experiences that text as itself historically conditioned and vulnerable to criticism. Arnold remains a powerful, although imperfect, example of a self-reflexive criticism that resists the reductions of ideology.

I hope that the *movement* of my own essay exemplifies the non-ideological critical spirit that I counterpose to ideology. It is not enough to value Arnold or any other thinker. One must point out the places where the movement of his critical spirit is arrested. I have no trouble imagining a critical reader finding such places in my own writing. The existence of such places is the raison d'etre of the ongoing project of criticism. It does not mean, however, that ideology is everywhere. It does mean that our intellectual autonomy and freedom have their limits.

CHAPTER FOUR

The Abandoned Legacy of the
New York Intellectuals

The New York intellectuals emerged in the 1930s in reaction to the Stalinism of the American Communist Party. Their main journal was *Partisan Review*, which originated in the John Reed Club under the editorship of William Phillips and Phillip Rahv. When Phillips and Rahv dissociated themselves from the party, they took the journal with them and established its independent existence. *Partisan Review* evolved from an anti-Stalinism with Trotskyist sympathies into a liberalism that took a hard line toward the Communist and fellow-traveling views of a significant portion of the liberally oriented educated class. (According to Richard Hofstadter, after World War II *Partisan Review* became "the house organ of the American intellectual community.")[1] During the 1960s, the journal veered from the course it had taken and held through the 1940s and 1950s and opened its pages to writers radicalized, politically and culturally, by the Civil Rights movement and the war in Vietnam. But the sixties proved to be an aberrant interlude in the life of the journal and the New York intellectuals. The seventies marked a return to their original inspiration.

Commentary, which began in 1945 under the auspices of the American Jewish Committee, had a comparable (although by no means identical) evolution, for it shared with *Partisan Review* virtually the same constituency of writers and readers. The New York intellectuals were not all New Yorkers, and they were mostly, but not exclusively, Jewish. New York was their main geographical site, although it was possible to be a New York intellectual in spirit and in practice through association with the journals and at the same time to identify oneself with another city, as Saul Bellow did with Chicago. The New York intellectuals belonged to a fraternity of intellect and sensibility that I will try to characterize in the pages that follow.

I am not writing the history of the New York intellectuals or revising the histories that have been written by historians like Alexander Bloom, Terry Cooney, and Alan Wald, although as will become clear I have a quarrel with some of Wald's conclusions. My purpose is to give an account of the essential political and cultural burden of the thought of the New York intellectuals in the forties and the fifties and to offer an explanation of why their legacy has been ignored by the contemporary literary academy.

In the lexicon of New York intellectuals, "academic" has always been an antonym of "intellectual." The second-rate, the mediocre, and the pedantic find their home in the academy. By contrast, the New York intellectuals believed themselves to be invigorated by their life in the great city, outside the walls of the academy. The inimical relationship between the New York intellectuals and the academy provides an insight into the character and culture of both parties.

The academic credentials of the New York intellectuals and

their view of academic requirements are revealing. A number of them (Jew and Gentile alike) never obtained advanced academic degrees. I have in mind Phillip Rahv, Fred Dupee, and Dwight Macdonald, among others. In some ways this turned out to be an advantage. It permitted them to pursue their intellectual and cultural interests free of disabling academic constraints: disciplinary barriers, scholarly apparatus, pedantic prose. From their beginnings, one finds a refreshing audacity in the pages of *Partisan Review* and *Commentary*, a sense of unaccountability to examiners, referees and degree-conferrers. This is not to say that the New York intellectuals never held academic jobs. Lionel Trilling taught at Columbia, as did Richard Chase and Fred Dupee, who never got beyond a B.A. Philip Rahv, the autodidact without a high school diploma or a B.A., taught at Brandeis University. Their teaching and writing, however, did not express themselves in the conventional academic channels.

The presence of Trilling, Chase, and Dupee at the annual convention of the Modern Languages Association, the professional organization of teachers and scholars of language and literature, is inconceivable. The association represented in their minds what was most academically conventional in literary studies, and they conveyed this attitude toward their students by never recommending participation in the activities of the organization or of comparable organizations. The result was that their students were never effectively socialized in the profession. Trilling chose to teach in the College rather than in the Graduate School because he had little affinity for the kinds of career-justifying specializations that were in vogue. The College provided a better forum for the larger cultural, political and literary issues that occupied him and his fellow New York intellectuals. Trilling did teach in the Graduate School and he directed dissertations, including mine, but graduate school was hardly his natural habitat. Which is not to say that Trilling and his colleagues did not feel comfortable in an academic environment. The fact is that the high academic tone of Columbia during the 1940s and 1950s (before the onslaught of the 1960s), its neo-

Victorian civility, was not only congenial to men like Trilling and Jacques Barzun, they positively cultivated it in their relationship with students and, I would guess, with colleagues. My own recollection of the experience of the Columbia atmosphere during the early 1950s is that my college mates and I were both impressed and oppressed.

The social ethos of Columbia should caution us against taking the academic-intellectual opposition at face value. It is in part an exercise in mythmaking. But the distinction is not without substance, and it concerns the question of the content of intellectual work. The New York intellectuals were interested in ideas of public significance, not confined within disciplinary boundaries. There were, to be sure, differences in tone and approach among them. Trilling's high style, filled with practiced hesitations, was in sharp contrast to Rahv's pugnacious polemical style. But intellectually and politically they were on the same terrain.

The paradox of Columbia for its undergraduates was its "non-academic" intellectual seriousness (in the sense in which New York intellectuals distinguished the intellectual from the academic). I remember my disappointment at the difference between the dreary scholarly fare of graduate school at Columbia and the intellectual passions in the college, and I recall the culture shock of discovering that the profession of literature at no less an institution than the University of Chicago, where I taught during the early 1960s, had nothing to do with the issues of politics and culture that were inextricably entwined in our education at Columbia.

So, when William Phillips and Philip Rahv, editors of *Partisan Review*, speak of the academic as "a quality of style marginal to important literary problems: a pedantic treatment of minor ideas with the emphasis placed on 'data' rather than on analysis," they are pointing to what they see as the failure of scholars to make their work relevant to contemporary issues of politics and culture.[2] When Clement Greenberg in more scathing language identifies the academic with *kitsch*, we detect an unargued animus against the academic that provokes a question about motive. "If kitsch is the watering down of the new, then self-evidently, all kitsch is academic, and conversely, all that's academic is kitsch. For what is called the academic as such no longer has an independent existence, but has become the stuffed shirt front for kitsch."[3] Is this antiacademicism sour grapes, a reflection of the disenfranchisement of the Jewish intellectual by the academy? The substantial presence of Jews in the academy is, as we all know, a comparatively recent phenomenon: Lionel Trilling and Harry Levin were the first Jewish tenured professors of English in the history of Columbia and Harvard, respectively. It would not be unnatural for the New York intellectuals to take their revenge for being excluded. I suspect, however, that they genuinely experienced a sense of superiority toward the academic. Was it justified?

One of their own, Sidney Hook, had a severely critical view of his fellow New York intellectuals, although not from an academic perspective. Writing in 1987, Hook remarks: "I never thought much of the intellectual sophistication of the editors of *Partisan Review*. . . . In the early years they were largely ignorant of or indifferent to American traditions."[4] Hook characterizes Rahv, who was the dominant personality of the journal, as "primarily a political man . . . who never expressed his appreciation for, no less delight in, the intrinsic properties of things" and who "never gave signs of enjoying an argument for its own sake, a story or poem or work of art for its form or craftsmanship, a person for his character or personality."[5] Hook singles out William Barrett as "the only trained mind among the editors of *PR*, the only one who could appreciate an argument in its own terms, and who recognized what constituted relevant evidence, and so forth."[6] The memoirs of Hook, Lionel Abel, Phillips, and Barrett are remarkable for their unflattering recollections of their colleagues. They testify to a collective cultural achievement, but the impression of personal dislikes, of mutual recriminations for unkindness, betrayals, political mistakes is very powerful. They were a quarrelsome and disagreeable (Jewish?) family, full of gifted, envious, competitive siblings who more often than not thought ill of one another. Hook's strictures about Rahv are exaggerations. I knew Rahv well in the last decade of his life (he died in 1973), knew him as a political man, a keen strategist in literary politics, but also as a reader and lover of books who could discourse impressively on James and Dostoevsky. But Hook's comments do point to intellectual limitations in the antiacademic stance of the New York intellectuals. *Partisan Review* was, and still is, a journal of opinion, of strong opinion, often brilliantly phrased but not worked out or developed to the point of disinterested (or should I say nonpartisan) knowledge. Its ideological origins in Marxism may have influenced its political character and aura, even when it challenged the cultural ideology of Marxism. The editors' hypersensitivity to pedantry and footnotes on occasion acted as an inhibition to the full development of an argument. And yet whatever its shortcomings, New York intellectual culture represented a powerful alternative to the academic way of life in the 1940s and 1950s.

The American academy has experienced a sea change since the 1960s. Russell Jacoby speaks of a "Marxist cultural revolution . . . taking place in American universities."[7] "Marxist cultural revolution" is not entirely accurate. Marxism is only one component of a pervasive radicalization of the literary academy, which we find in the New Historicism, deconstruction, ideology critique, cultural studies, a concern with gender issues. Anyone familiar with the history of radical politics would not be surprised by internecine conflicts in which one radical orientation (e.g., Marxism) would find another orientation (e.g., New Historicism) wanting in genuine radicalism. In any event, given the change in the character of the literary academy, one might think that the New York intellectuals might have finally found an audience. Why is it, then, that the recent academic interest in ideological issues and culture studies, for example, draws so little upon the work of Clement Greenberg, Harold Rosenberg, Dwight MacDonald among others? In order to answer the question, we need to understand the literary and cultural politics of the New York intellectuals: what they stood for and what they were against. Much of what follows is already familiar to readers who have followed the history of *Partisan Review* and *Commentary* or who have read the books of Cooney, Jacoby, and Wald, among others. What I hope to reveal in my account are the reasons why the legacy of the New York intellectual has been lost on the contemporary academy.

Within the literary academy of the 1940s and 1950s, a struggle took place between the traditional practitioners of philological and historical scholarship and the New Critics, who affirmed the aesthetic autonomy of the text, in effect making all extra aesthetic considerations of history, politics, even culture irrelevant. Practice did not always square with theory, so one can find evidences of historical perspectives in the New Criticism, but the idea of aesthetic autonomy powerfully conditioned academic literary discourse in the academy. The authority for this view came from the triumphant modernist literature of Eliot, Joyce, and Pound, the legatees of nineteenth-century aestheticism. Modernist art was to be a bastion against the squalors of modernity. The New York intellectuals stood in an odd relation to this conflict.

Growing up in a political world in New York, conscious of political event and implication in their adolescent years (one has only to read the memoirs of Barrett, Hook, Phillips, Abel, and Irving Howe), they could hardly be expected to suspend their political consciousness in the presence of works of art.[8] They also responded to James and Eliot and to European writers like Proust and Kafka. But they were interested always in the political and cultural dimension, in the historic moment represented by the art. (I should add that the historical perspective of the New York intellectuals, formed as it was by Marxism, was worlds apart from traditional historical scholarship.) Aesthetic evaluation and the historical perspective were different from each other, but not mutually exclusive. Politics was not irrelevant to art; they existed (or could exist) in a fruitful tension with each other. The New York intellectuals shared with their New Critical rivals a powerful antipathy to the ideological subordination of art to politics. Irving Howe's statement about the political novel is exemplary.

The political novel—I have in mind its "ideal" form—is peculiarly a work of internal tensions. To be a novel at all, it must contain the usual representation of human behavior and feeling; yet it must also absorb into its stream of movement the hard and perhaps insoluble pellets of modern ideology. The novel deals with moral sentiments, with passions and emotions; it tries, above all, to capture the quality of concrete experience. Ideology, however, is abstract, as it must be, and therefore likely to be recalcitrant whenever an attempt is made to incorporate it into the novel's stream of sensuous impression. The conflict is inescapable: the novel tries to confront experience in its immediacy and closeness, while ideology is by its nature general and inclusive. Yet it is precisely from this conflict that the political novel gains its interest and takes on the aura of high drama.[9]

If art exposes the abstractness of ideology, a political perspective might reveal the limitations of the aesthetic life. Thus in 1962 William Phillips spoke of a division between modern literature and a rational and positive politics as something that must be maintained: "It now looks as though a radical literature and a radical politics must be kept apart. For radical politics of the modern variety has really served as an antidote to literature. The moral hygiene, the puritanism, the benevolence—all the virtues that sprout on the left—work like a cure for the perverse and morbid idealism of the modern writer."[10] The relations between literature and politics may change, but the view of that relationship as a dialectic, a fruitful antagonism or a collaboration in which each term preserves its identity was, in the view of the New York intellectuals, at the very heart of the critical enterprise.

What made the New York literary perspective so powerful at the time of its ascendancy was its double capacity to value the work of art as a work of art and to see its political significance, even when it was ostensibly apolitical or antipolitical. The powers of art (which include its political power) depended on its resistance to ideological subordination. A typical target of criticism was *The New Masses*, which, according to James Farrell "had [in Terry Cooney's paraphrase] introduced political standards into their criticism that produced vulgar, oversimplified and irrelevant judgments."[11] Not that Phillips and Rahv, especially in their radical phase, would allow for the absolute autonomy of art. They were critics of writers who "seek to assimilate the Joyce-Eliot sensibility without a clear revolutionary program."[12] Marxism and modernist literature shared, in their view, a radical critical relation to the world and a universalist outlook, but they were always vigilant in their resistance to any attempt to make literature into a mere servile activity.

Literary academic discourse today can be understood as a rejection of both the New Criticism and the criticism practiced by the New York intellectuals. The New Critical idea of a literary work, coherent and self-sufficient, interpretable in its own terms, is a disreputable, if not a discredited, idea. The tension between art and politics, sponsored by the New York intellectuals, has been dissolved. If the work of art is no longer privileged, no longer to be distinguished from any other item in the general culture (and here culture is to be understood in its anthropological sense), then art loses whatever cultural authority it possessed. Art, like any other cultural expression (journalism, advertising and so on), belongs to an ideological formation that it cannot escape. The attempt to view a work of art in aesthetic terms reveals the work of aesthetic ideology: the aesthetic element is a mystification of power motives that may take a class or race or gender form. All sophisticated literary discussion (under the new dispensation) is ideology critique: that is, an exercise in demystification. (I am referring to New Historicism, radical feminist criticism, certain versions of deconstruction.) The new ideology critique does not have to urge the subordination of art to politics because in its view all art is always already ideological. The issue, then, is the acknowledgement of this putative truth.

The ideologues of the 1930s and 1940s could be characterized as intellectually crude and vulgar. Not so the contemporary variety, who are given to a linguistically inspired pyrotechnical academic prose. Underneath the abstractions and sophistications of this prose, however, one discerns the kind of ideological reflex that the New York intellectuals devoted so much time and space to attacking. It would be a misrepresentation to say that the difference between the New York intellectuals and the academic vanguard (spawned, I believe, during the 1960s) is simply a political difference: that is, the difference between right and left, between disillusioned time-serving conservatives and young radicals determined to change the world. The New York perspective that I am sketching coexisted at one time with a Marxist perspective in politics. It even had the support of Leon Trotsky. For the New York intellectuals serious art was high art. As Marxism lost its hold on them in the 1950s, writers like Dwight Macdonald, Clement Greenberg, and Leslie Fiedler devoted themselves to the cause of high culture, elaborating a hierarchy of high-, middle-, and lowbrow in the cultural life.[13] Much of their critical energy was directed against the middlebrow (see, for instance, Dwight MacDonald's devastating attack on James Gould Cozzens's *By Love Possessed*).[14] Something of the ideological passion of their abandoned Marxism informed their excessively hierarchical conception of culture: the enemy is the bourgeois, the cultural philistine of the middle class.

However radical the New York intellectuals were in politics, they exempted culture from democratic and egalitarian standards. The radical cultural populism of contemporary literary academic politics was utterly inimical to the cultural politics of the New York intellectuals. The famous Russian revolutionary of the 1840s, Alexander Herzen, once spoke of the authority of reason in a way that the New York intellectuals might have spoken of culture: "the submission of reason [substitute culture] to a majority vote . . . [is] the expression of a *democratic* untruth,"[15] a remark the New York intellectuals would have found congenial. One of the marks of postmodernism is its complete democratization of the cultural idea, its appropriation by the electoral process, or rather by an elite of radical populists who speak in the name of the people.

Cultural populism represents the attempts of women, ethnic and racial minorities to achieve cultural enfranchisement. Ethnicity is the new populism. Cultural production comes to be valued not for its aesthetic or intellectual distinction but for its representative powers. The cultural work of minorities is, so to speak, elected to a new cultural parliament. The New York Jewish intellectuals also faced the problem of cultural enfranchisement, but they enacted a different solution to the problem. They looked for enfranchisement not through the validation of their ethnicity but through entry into the already existing universality of European culture. They identified themselves with internationalist and cosmopolitan values. Their cosmopolitanism was consistent with the fate of the Jew in diaspora, his or her role as a wanderer among nations. It expressed itself in the internationalist outlook of both Marxism and modernism.

The identification with cosmopolitan values is itself part of a venerable (although contested) Jewish tradition that has its provenance in the Enlightenment. The *maskilim* identified the Jewish mind with a universalist rationalism. They sought to overcome the ghettoized existence of Jewish European life, an externally imposed existence with which certain tendencies of Jewish thought and feeling unfortunately conspired. This is not to say that the New York Jewish intellectuals were consciously assimilationist: their sensibility, wit, manners, and accent retained what might be called a "Jewish character." Even the famous breakthrough of Jewish writers onto the main stage of American literature initiated by Saul Bellow's *Adventures of Augie March* (1953) was less an assertion of Jewish identity (more accurately of parochial identity) than an *identification* with American life. When Augie March declares who he is at the outset of the novel ("I am American, Chicago born"), he is asserting his Americanness. The roots of *The Adventures of Augie March* are in *The Adventures of Huckleberry Finn*, not the Yiddish writers of the past, although Bellow's command of the Yiddish idiom would contribute a new vernacular to American literature.

The idea of a world or national literature beyond ethnicity should not exclude the diverse energies of ethnic life. But those energies require the justification of art. The fact of ethnicity does not in itself qualify the work. The breakthrough of American Jewish literature in the 1950s meant that Jewish writing had come of age and that there was now a larger American audience prepared to read it. Certain Jewish critics fostered the myth that the breakthrough *one-sidedly* reflected the maturing of American culture. According to editors of an anthology of American Jewish writing, the " 'breakthrough' meant not that the Jew has caught up with America. America has at long last caught up with the Jew. His search for identity is its search. Its quest for spiritual meaning is his quest."[16] Behind this myth is an ideology of ethnicity that governs the contemporary cultural scene, for it ignores the necessity of Jewish writing to develop from the provinciality of the work of immigrant Yiddish writers to a self-reflective, even ironic maturity of the succeeding generation.

An act of cultural enfranchisement like the breakthrough of the American Jewish writer or the emergence of women and black writers as major presences on the cultural scene necessarily brings in its wake a neglected past: it reshapes our sense of tradition. One effect of the breakthrough of American Jewish writers has been the retrieval of Henry Roth's *Call It Sleep*, 1934, and Daniel Fuchs's Williamsburg Trilogy: *Summer in Williamsburg*, 1934; *Homage to Blenholt*, 1936; and *Low Company*, 1937. The crucial questions are: what do we declare of value in the past; Which works by Jews, blacks, and women do we value; and For what reasons? Do we recover a work because of some political or ethnic service that it performs or because of its aesthetic or intellectual character?

In the prevailing perspective, such a distinction becomes moot because of the assumed impossibility of separating the political and the aesthetic. Already in the early sixties, Ralph Ellison, the author of *Invisible Man*, responded to what he felt was pressure to parochialize him within a Negro literary tradition. He explains why he turned not to Richard Wright but to Hemingway for inspiration.

> Do you still ask why Hemingway was more important to me than Wright? Not because he was white, or more "accepted." But because

he appreciated the things of this earth which I love and which Wright was too driven or deprived or inexperienced to know: weather, guns, dogs, horses, love *and* hate and impossible circumstances which to the courageous and dedicated could be turned into benefits and victories. Because he wrote with such precision about the processes and techniques of daily living that I could keep myself and my brother alive during the 1937 Recession by following his descriptions of wing-shooting; because he knew the difference between politics and art and something of their true relationship for the writer. Because all that he wrote—and this is very important— was imbued with a spirit beyond the tragic with which I could feel at home, for it was very close to the feeling of the blues, which are, perhaps, as close as Americans can come to expressing the spirit of tragedy.[17]

Similarly for the American Jewish writer and critic, it has been a matter of artistic pride that the Jewishness of a work enter into a consideration of its meanings, but not of its power and value as a work of art.

The idea of a world literature or of cultural universality is, of course, deeply suspect these days. Cultural universalism we have been taught is no more than western civilization, an ideological mystification of cultural imperialism. Cultural ethnicity is one antidote. But the blind spot in such a view is that it can easily turn into provinciality. It is of course true that the West is not the world, but Western or European consciousness in its *most humane form* has shown an unequalled awareness of difference (anthropology, after all, is a Western discipline). To be locked into one's ethnicity is to be blind to the claims of others; to go beyond ethnicity in this sense is to expand one's consciousness of the world.

An Enlightenment perspective imposes on its exponents an obligation to express themselves in a style relatively free of technical jargon, although not at the expense of difficulty and complexity. In the spirit of the Enlightenment, the New York intellectuals thought of themselves as public intellectuals who reached out to an educated, unspecialized audience.[18] Such an audience is, of course, limited, hardly universal, but it is necessary to the mythology of the public intellectual that the potentiality of its appeal not be confined to any particular group, defined by a specialized learning. In contrast, contemporary academic prose, written by Marxist and other radical scholars, is often hermetic and jargon ridden, a far cry from the lucid prose of the New York intellectuals.

At issue in the debates about the appropriate style of intellectual discourse is the prestige of Enlightenment thought. If the Enlightenment is understood as the origin of a progressive tradition in which Marxism itself is a later manifestation, the vernacular becomes the prose of demystification and truth. But if the Enlightenment is understood as an originally progressive force turned reactionary, as the Frankfurt school had come to understand it, then the lucidity of the vernacular idiom becomes suspect, obscuring as it does the problematic relationship between language and reality. In *Writing Degree Zero*, Roland Barthes makes a case against what he conceives to be the mystifications of the transparent style of Enlightenment thought. Transparency is a deceiving strategy of the rising bourgeois class, which seeks to universalize its own particular interests. There is truth, I think, in the anti-Enlightenment view. A reader of *Notes from Underground* or *Heart of Darkness* cannot be unmoved by the impression of the facility and hubris of a vision in which Reason declares itself as master of the world. But the mystifications of a deified Reason hardly justifies a prose that deliberately darkens understanding and then claims to be itself an instrument of demystification.

Even Marxism, which in its classic formulation owes a great deal to the Enlightenment has been contaminated by the contemporary reaction against it, both in its content and its style. Contemporary academic Marxism has lost its universalist character, becoming another parochialism, a kind of vested interest, another "ethnicity" so to speak. And it has insulated itself from political reality. Marxism in the Althusserian idiom has nothing to tell us about contemporary realities. There is an extraordinary incongruity between contemporary American academic Marxism and the global disenchantment with Marxism. Academic Marxism would seem to illustrate the New Historicist view that all subversion is to a large degree illusory, that radical ideas are easily coopted by the establishment they are supposed to subvert. The very abstractness and hermeticism of the ideas, one might add, make them innocuous as revolutionary ideas. A never-never land of conferences in which political reality is rarely engaged, academic Marxism has never faced the contradictions (to use one of its favorite tropes) between its professed concern for the oppressed and the inhumanity of the social and cultural systems that have been constructed in its name.

The Marxism of the New York intellectuals in all its heterogeneity was a sensitive barometer of the political changes in the world. To be sure, the New York intellectuals had their follies and abstractions, but they were engaged with the real world as contemporary academics are not. I don't want to misrepresent them as activists. As early as 1940 Trilling expressed with an Arnoldian pessimism the social power of even the most persuasive criticism when he conceived "the critical task as the work of a very small group [in which] our possibility of action [is] suspended by events [and] our relations with the future [are] dark and dubious."[19] In a sense, activism was inimical to the truth telling to which the New York intellectuals were committed. The ethos of New York intellectual culture reflected a tension between partisanship and a disinterested desire to disengage the truth from partisan efforts to distort it in the interests of a cause.

In his study of the New York intellectuals, Alan Wald compares the views of Philip Rahv and Terry Eagleton for the purpose of contrasting what he believes to be deluded pragmatic (experience-based) Marxism with true Marxist epistemology. Wald faults Rahv for separating ideology and experience. He endorses Eagleton's view that experience is "precisely ideology's homeland, connoting the way one senses, feels or receives ordinary life activity; experience is another word for everyday consciousness, imbued with the norms and values of class society and its rulers."[20] Wald, I think, conflates (without knowing it) two meanings of *ideology*, that is, ideology in the anthropological sense (Eagleton's formulation) and ideology in the sense of false consciousness (Rahv's Marxist understanding of the word). Eagleton's own formulation, I should add, suggests a confusion in the matter. Although, as I pointed out earlier, Eagleton subscribes to an anthropological sense of ideology (a way of life) in which questions of truth and falsity do not or should not arise, he never frees himself from an incompatible conception of ideology as false consciousness, imposed on society by the upper class.

Wald goes on to praise Eagleton's conception of the relationship between ideology and experience as providing a genuine basis for art "as a potential liberator from ideological illusion." But if ideology is as pervasive as Wald and Eagleton claim, what is it that preserves art itself from a disabling ideological contamination? How can art expose illusion, if it is itself permeated by ideology? Wald clearly means to suggest that it is Eagleton, not Rahv, who has a keen grasp of experience. One wonders, however, how keen or direct that grasp can be if it is always mediated by ideology. I suspect in the cases of both Wald and Eagleton the working of the academic mind in its mistrust of the pragmatic and the experiential. The claim for a clear-seeing Orwell or Naipaul is simply declared to be ideological mystification. Moreover, there is no sense in Wald or Eagleton (or in poststructuralist discourse) of the freedom of art, of its constitutive beauty-making powers. The double effect of failing to distinguish between the claims of art and politics (as the New York intellectuals did) is to impoverish our understanding of both art and politics.

It may be impossible, given the present disposition of energies and forces on the cultural scene, to revive the cult of high art. The cosmopolitan model of Jewish ethnicity may seem irrelevant to the ethnic insurgencies in contemporary American culture, but it would be, I think, a mistake not to allow it to be part of the cultural debate—unless we are content to be historicist fatalists who have lost faith in the productive possibilities of such a debate.

CHAPTER FIVE

Kenneth Burke Revisited

For the New York intellectuals, Kenneth Burke was an example of the liberal weakness for Stalinism in the decades of the 1930s and 1940s. Recently, he has been adopted by deconstructionists as a precursor of their own interest in rhetoric and by those who are critical of what they regard as the apolitical character of deconstruction. Frank Lentricchia, in particular, has turned to Burke as an outstanding example from the past of a politically engaged vernacular critic. My own view is that much of the criticism of Burke by the New York intellectuals has been ungenerous and that both deconstruction and its left-wing critics (or at least Frank Lentricchia) have misappropriated Burke to suit their own ideological agendas. Burke is an original, not to be pigeonholed. I turn to Burke, because long before the current obsession with ideology critique he was acutely aware of both its appeal and its perils. He also anticipated our present preoccupation with the dissolution of the distinction between high and low culture and with the perspectival character of our knowledge and the attendant problem of communication among perspectives. He had his inadequacies and failures (who hasn't?), but unlike contemporary ideology critics and perspectivists Burke was admirably responsive to the need to respect the spirit of a work even as he redescribed it in his own terms; indeed, redescription (to use the Rortyian term) was for Burke a way of reviving, not subverting, the text. He also understood that a world constituted of perspectives required that human beings find ways of communicating among them. Moreover, among critics of the Left in the 1930s and 1940s, he is as far as I know uniquely sensitive to the ineradicable religious or theological aspect of our cultural experience. His work shows us what we have lost in our passion for desacralization.

Nothing human is alien to Kenneth Burke. He is the least confined of modern critics. It is not simply that he writes about everything: he tries to include everything within a system or systems of explanation that have the effect of conservation. In the narrow political sense, Burke is by no means a conservative, and yet one might say that he is the most "conservational" of critics. The trajectory of Burke's career from the first collection of essays *Counter-Statement* to *The Rhetoric of Religion* is a movement of increasing encompassment of all branches of knowledge: literature, sociology, philosophy, linguistics, theology, and so forth. "Branches of knowledge" is misleading, because of his peculiarly idiosyncratic appropriation of them.

How to characterize this most encompassing, yet most personal, of critics? The question has been raised, particularly by writers hostile to his enterprise, about whether indeed Burke qualifies as a literary critic. Thus Marius Bewley, one of his severest critics, has noted "how easily, without an exacting critical conscience, Burke's theory moves through art to propaganda, how easily the literary

merges into the revolutionary critic."[1] The occasion for the charge
is an extended passage in *Attitudes Toward History*, of which the following sentences should serve: "Our own program, as literary
critic, is to integrate technical criticism with social criticism (propaganda and didactic) by taking the allegiance to the symbol of
authority as our subject. . . . And since the whole purpose of a 'revolutionary' critic is to contribute to a change in allegiance to the
symbols of authority, we maintain our role as 'propagandist' by
keeping this subject forever uppermost in our concerns."[2] Burke's
role as revolutionary critic may be only a phase or aspect of his total
performance, but it is taken to be expressive of a characteristic disposition in the performance. It is evidence for Bewley and others of
Burke's incapacity "to conceive of literary criticism as a central discipline."[3]

It should be noted that Bewley's response is to an early work in
which the Marxist element (a product of the 1930s) seemed much
more prominent than it does now in retrospect. One is indeed surprised by the Marxist element, coming to *Attitudes Toward History*
after a reading of late work like *A Grammar of Motives* and *The
Rhetoric of Religion*. Bewley's point, however, is not to charge Burke
with being a Marxist, but to show how his ecumenicism, his catholic
embrace of all disciplines, his pragmatic inclination to turn everything to use puts in question his role as a literary critic.

What is at work is an assumption, shared by Bewley, Ransom,
Tate and other modernists, about the separate integrity of the disciplines and in particular the literary or aesthetic disciplines. New
Critics resisted the contamination of discussions of poems and even
novels by political or moral considerations. Political and moral
themes were interesting only insofar as they were transformed into
literary structures. The effort of separation and purification of the
disciplines belongs to a classic modernist desire to overcome
Victorian moralizing and a Marxian politicizing of literature. The
effort at separation has proved problematic. A rigorous scrutiny of
the literary or the aesthetic shows how often the term conceals
moral, political and spiritual interests. The literary is itself an amal-

gam. Consider, for instance, Bewley's praise of Burke, for whom "poetry becomes, not a segregated experience, but an experience at one with all human action. . . . Poetry is therefore seen to be ethical, and of the deepest influence in shaping our structures of orientation."[4] The issue is not whether the critic preserves, so to speak, his literary chastity, but whether his sensibility remains literary while responding to the amalgam that constitutes literature. Burke does not put in question the very idea of literature as some poststructuralists have done, but his lack of aesthetic purism leads to the kind of disciplinary interactions in his work that make him a modernist in a sense in which his New Critical peers were not.

Burke transgresses with impunity disciplinary boundaries; he also appropriates subjects traditionally deemed unworthy of serious intellectual and aesthetic consideration. R. P. Blackmur's charge, picked up by others, that Burke's method "could be applied with equal fruitfulness to Shakespeare, or Marie Corelli, and Dashiell Hammett"[5] (since the evaluative element seems to be missing) presupposes a distinction between higher and lower forms of cultural life that Burke did not explicitly disavow, but in practice disregarded. He is a forerunner of those critics, now legion, who engage all forms of cultural expression with an unin-vidious interest, at once aesthetic and sociological. The weakening, if not dissolution, of the high-low distinction makes it possible for critics now not only to discover the sociological conditions shared by a variety of artistic and cultural forms but to consider as well aesthetic value in popular forms of cultural life. Arnold, as one might expect, was for Burke a bête noire.

Unlike his contemporaries (Ransom, Tate, Blackmur, among others) Burke is not to be approached *simply* as a literary critic, analyzing individual works of literature. It is not, however, enough to say that literary criticism is one among many of the activities that Burke engages in. He is not an eclectic of disciplines. He is a critic with systematic ambitions, although I think it inaccurate to represent him as a systematic critic. His work is marked by a tension between the effort to systematize and the need to resist the stultifying consequences of such an effort. Indeed, Burke's work gives the impression of waywardness rather than the rigor of step-by-step construction characteristic of the system building of, say, Northrop Frye. We can see the contrary tendencies in Burke's thought in his definition of man, from which many of his ideas and observations flow. "Man is a symbol-using animal, the inventor of the negative, separated from his natural condition by instruments of his own making, goaded by the spirit of hierarchy and rotten with perfection."[6] The definition suggests a number of affinities and inspirations. Man as a symbol-making animal evokes the American pragmatist George Mead and the anthropologists, Leslie White and Alfred H. Kroeber. In stressing the separation from the natural (elsewhere he will speak of transcendence), we should also recognize the secularizing humanist (a legatee of the nineteenth century) interested in preserving spiritual ambition in a materializing world. Hierarchy and perfection evoke Burke's affinities with the classical tradition and in particular with Aristotelian teleology. The definition also suggests the skepticism that informs Burke's work: the idea of the *negative*, the problematic *separation* from the natural condition, the *rot* of perfection, that threatens all hierarchies.

In *Permanence and Change*, Burke makes it clear that he wants to unsettle things, not tidy them into a neat system. He is concerned with "how an 'orientation' (or general view of reality) takes form. How such a system of interpretation, by its very scope and thoroughness, interferes with its own revision. Why terms like 'escape,' 'scapegoat mechanism,' 'pleasure principle,' and 'rationalization' should be used skeptically and grudgingly."[7] No interpretation is secure: "we may also interpret our interpretations."[8] Burke's desire to keep things open, to question the terms of the structures and activities he scrutinizes is homeopathic (cathartic) rather than destructive. In his first book *Counter-Statement* he contrasts platonic censorship to Aristotle's homeopathic "lightning rod" poetics which he prefers. "Lightning rods are designed, not to suppress danger, but to draw it into harmless channels."[9] Skepticism may be viewed as a way of venting (not suppressing) dangerous energies, so that the work of structure-making can continue.

But Burke is also keenly aware of the radical and corrosive tendency in modern art, which he finds in Mann and Gide, writers whom he admires but about whom he feels a certain ambivalence. "There is an art, a questioning art, still cluttered with the merest conveniences of thinking, a highly fluctuant thing often turning against itself and its own best discoveries. How far it will go, how well it can maintain its characters, I should not venture to calculate. But working in the traditions of such art are two conscientious, or corrupt writers, Thomas Mann and Andre Gide."[10] Burke's commitment to the constitutive impulse in human life sets him apart from the tendency of modernist thought to demystify all structures, to deflate pretensions, to dispel illusions.

Demystification is the most powerful method of the modern intellectual's will to power, and Burke is a most penetrating critic of modernist debunking. What he tries above all to do is to account for the motives which impel men to construct and constitute the structures that fill the space of *human* life.

> Our resistance to a purely "debunking" vocabulary of motives is made clear if we imagine a thinker who chose to "debunk" such a motive as "solidarity." There are unquestionably ways in which one may "cash in on" it, in the purely selfish sense of the term—but if *all* acts of "solidarity" were interpreted in the light of this possibility, its "reality" would be dissolved out of existence . . . quite as Democritus' atomism resolved the gods out of existence. . . . Those who cooperate with the help of this concept must leave its "euphemistic" nature as a motive intact.[11]

Even a debunker like Freud acknowledges the necessity and value of "mystery and mystification." "Every man has his 'secret,' an awe too deep for the boldness and shrewdness of rational verbalization. There is the 'trembling veil' of sleep, which he cannot draw without risk."[12] Debunking works against such understanding, and indeed, as Burke cunningly suggests, is susceptible of the same demystifying treatment it accords all other activities, structures and motives. "While leading you to watch his act of destruction at one point, the 'unmasker' is always furtively building at another point, and by his prestidigitation, he can forestall accurate observation of his own moves."[13]

How does Burke the anti-debunker avoid a falsifying mystification, surely a bad thing in the realm of thought? Sidney Hook believes that Burke is a mystifier, and he discovers it in particular in Burke's fellow-traveling communism. Hook focuses on Burke's habit of finding a central metaphor in a work or action in order to understand its achievement. He cites the instance of Burke's review of Henri Barbusse's idolatrous biography of Stalin. Burke characterizes the biography as a "public monument," in effect extenuating if not justifying the extraordinary mystification and falsification of Stalin's life by Barbusse. Hook mischievously suggests "the dung hill" as another appropriate metaphor for the book. "Why one metaphor rather than another?," Hook asks.[14] He implies that the metaphor is not adventitious, that is, it reflects a political allegiance to communism, and communism in its Stalinist version.

There is certainly substantial evidence in Burke's early work of that allegiance. But the instance of Barbusse's *Stalin* is in a sense a diversion from a full and generous understanding of what Burke is up to. He does a similar thing with Hitler's *Mein Kampf* and one can hardly impute Nazi motives to him. Burke's way is always to enter into the spirit of the work, to try to grasp its rhetorical, that is to say its persuasive power. (Who would deny the persuasiveness of *Mein Kampf*?) We need to keep in mind that rhetoric is one of Burke's main subjects and that mystification is inescapably implicated in rhetorical performance. The issue is not necessarily truth, but belief. Burke means to examine the myriad ways in which language leads people to conviction and action. His virtuosity both as rhetorician and as student of rhetoric consists in his extraordinary awareness of "the endless catalogue of terministic screens"[15] in and through which human beings live. "Screen," of course, is an image of concealment and mystification, but the image can be one of discovery and illumination as well.

> If you decree by secular prayer that man is "essentially" a warrior (as did Nietzsche) you may then proceed, by casuistic stretching, to discern the warlike ingredient present even in love. If on the contrary you legislated to the effect that man is essentially a communicant, you could discern the co-operative ingredient present "essentially" even in war. Capitalism is "essentially" competitive (on this point, both opponents and proponents agree). But despite this essence, we note the presence of many non-competitive ingredients (there are many examples of true "partnership") in the competitive struggle.[16]

Burke's effort is not to expose in a pejorative sense what is behind the screen, but rather to explain the rhetorical power of the screen. Burke does not hold the sophistic view that rhetoric is indifferent to the question of truth and falsity and therefore must be demystified. What he seeks to do is to uncover the truth that makes a rhetorical statement persuasive: for instance, "the warlike ingredient present in love." Burke in effect revives the ancient reputation of casuistry, which the Shorter Oxford Dictionary defines in its noncontemptible sense as "the science, art, or reasoning of the casuist; that part of Ethics which resolves cases of conscience, applying the general rules of religion and morality to particular instances which disclose special circumstances, or conflicting duties."

The danger of terministic screens and casuistic stretching is a relativism with truth, whatever it may be, as the casualty. The difficulty arises (and here Hook's criticism is relevant) in the indiscriminateness with which Burke treats all intellectual and imaginative structures, literary, philosophical, political. It is not enough for a critic to provide a metaphor for the intention of Barbusse's *Stalin* or Hitler's *Mein Kampf*, he must evaluate it in moral terms as well. He must *transcend,* to use a favorite Burke term, the merely rhetorical.

But Burke's insufficiency in the case of certain texts, those with momentous political consequences, does not undermine the essential value of Burke's resistance to debunking as a pervasive activity. Indeed, it suggests that Hook and others have exaggerated the significance of Burke's allegiance to Marxism, since he is after all so antipathetic to its demystifying spirit.

What distinguishes Burke is not so much his allegiance to a particular "symbol of authority" as his negative capacity for sympathetically grasping allegiances to a variety of symbols of authority to the point of undermining his moral credibility. As between Marx, the dyslogist and Carlyle, the eulogist, for example, Burke remains suspended in indecision as if he wants it both ways: the mystery and the "truth" that lies concealed beneath the mystery, without evaporating the mystery. In a discussion of Carlyle's "Philosophy of Clothes" in *Sartor Resartus*, Burke says that he has "not been trying to abolish, or debunk, or refute, or even to 'approve with reservations.' Above all, we are not trying to decide whether mystery should be considered dyslogistically, as with Marx, or eulogistically, as with Carlyle. For we need not decide here whether there should or should not be reverence (hence 'mystification')."[17] If not here, certainly elsewhere and in many places, Burke almost always prefers the eulogist. (More recently, Roland Barthes in *Mythologies* has in a way that recalls Burke addressed himself to the poverty of demystification, lamenting "the drift between the object and its demystification, powerless to render its wholeness.")[18]

Burke's stance against debunking is consistent with the role of literary critic. While debunking may be an essential activity of sociology, for instance, it is more often than not inimical to the practice of literary criticism. What counts above all for the literary critic is the language that constitutes the work. Words are at once the surface and the reality of literature, to which the demystifier's suspicious view of the spoken or written word is inimical. Burke shares with his modern contemporaries a belief in language as the essential subject of literary study. In contrast to his contemporaries (Brooks, Ransom, Empson, Tate), who focus most of their critical activity on individual works, lyric poems in particular, in order to discover the ambiguities and paradoxes of language and the sui generis character of the individual work, Burke attempts a more systematic understanding of the workings of language.

The master discipline for the study of language is theology. It is an emergent idea throughout Burke's late work and receives its most complete expression in *The Rhetoric of Religion.* "A close study of theology and its forms will provide us with good insight into the nature of language itself."[19] In *Language as Symbolic Action,* Burke writes: "Everything that can be said about 'God' has its analogue in something that can be said about *language.* And just as theorizing about God leads to so-called 'negative theology,' so theorizing about language heads in the all-importance of the Negative."[20] Theology is not simply the language of human transcendence, it reveals the telic, transcending properties of language itself. Burke refers to a word like honor as a god term, because it represents an aspiration toward a kind of perfection.[21] The ultimate term, of course, is God himself. Analogy may be too weak a term to describe the relationship between theology and language. For Burke theology represents the essence of language itself.

Theology, of course, cannot be reduced to language. Thus the study of language requires another name, for which Burke provides the neologism, logology. And he specifies the difference between theology and logology. "Logology fails to offer grounds for the *perfection* of promises and threats that theology allows for."[22] Burke's secularizing project, a version of the secularizing humanism of the nineteenth century, is distinguished by an attention to the rhetorical constitution of theology, a concern with the relation of the Word to words. As William Rueckert puts it: "Burke offers a logological ('naturalistic and empirical,' he calls it) explanation of the Christian drama of creation, disobedience, fall, expulsion, expiation and redemption which, from a theological point of view, is an extended reversed analogy since he moves from 'words' to the 'The Word'; or from the natural, verbal and socio-political to the supernatural as an analogical extension of the first three."[23] In *The Rhetoric of Religion,* Burke's main text is Augustine's *Confessions.* But

Burke should not be read as an apologist for Christian orthodoxy.
Although he works exclusively within a Christian framework (a radical unconsidered limitation to his logology), he attempts to
encompass and in a sense validate all the heretical and even anti-
nomian tendencies within the theological project and modern secular versions.

> There are, underlying the Church, many ingenious heresies so thor-
> oughly silenced by the sword that they survive only in the refutations
> of the faithful. There are subtle schemes deriving the best of human
> insight from Cain, or centering salvation upon the snake, or lauding
> the act of Judas Iscariot which procured for uneasy mankind a God
> as scapegoat. To look back upon them is to consider a wealth of
> antinomian enterprise expended in ways which seem excessive, trou-
> blesome, and unnecessary, their gratuity being surpassed only by the
> same qualities among the orthodox. But let one not be misled into
> thinking that the heresies have perished.[24]

Burke does not identify himself with any single tendency, orthodox
or heretical, or rather through a suspension of disbelief he is able
to identify himself at different times with all tendencies. This is what
is meant by "perspective by incongruity." Burke has been compared
to Coleridge for his philosophic range, but his closest affinity, it
seems to me, is with Keats, the "theorist" of negative capability.

For all the insights Burke's logology has offered, it has not
played a central role in contemporary literary discourse. The
advent of poststructuralism, in particular deconstruction, has
revived interest in Burke's logology. Burke anticipates the emphasis in deconstruction on logocentrism, but with a wholly different
intention. Whereas Burke attempts to show the ways in which language unfolds motives and constitutes structures, deconstruction
tries to undo structures and expose the illusoriness of motives [ori-
gins]. Burke represents a powerful modern version of the nineteenth-century higher criticism, which deconstruction with its powerful antitheological animus is trying to undo. The fact that Burke

commands respectful attention from poststructuralists and post-modernists is a sign not necessarily of agreement, but of similar pre-occupations. The difference between Burke and the postmod-ernists is nowhere more evident than in the contrast between him and Rorty. Whereas Burke tries to retrieve theology from its repres-sion in modern culture, Rorty's effort is to eradicate whatever ves-tiges of it exist through what he calls dedivinization. Burke's valu-ing of the theological is consistent with his mistrust of the debunk-ing spirit of modern culture.

The theological analogue represents Burke's distinctive contri-bution primarily to linguistic speculation. As a literary theorist and critic, Burke may be fairly characterized as neo-Aristotelian, although not of the Chicago school. He calls his version dramatism, which is composed of the pentad, "scene," "act," "agent," "agency," and "purpose." In *A Grammar of Motives*, in which each term is exposed in a separate chapter, Burke's interest is in the dramatistic implications of philosophy and reciprocally the philosophical implications of dramatism. His subjects are Aristotle, Aquinas, Spinoza, Leibnitz, and Kant, among others (in short, "The Philosophic Schools"). In Aristotelian fashion, Burke attempts to show how narrative unfolds the logic of an idea through time, "tem-porizes essence" in Burke's phrase.

> Thus the search for "logical" priority can, when translated into tem-poral, or narrative terms, be expressed in the imagery of "regression to childhood," or in other imagery or ideas of things past. This con-cern with the statement of essence in terms of *origins* (ancestry) [may be complemented by] the statement of essence in terms of *cul-minations* (where the narrative notion of "how it all ends up" does serve for the logically reductive notion of "what it all boils down to"). In either choice (the ancestral or the final) the narrative terminol-ogy provides for a *personalizing* of essence."[25]

Above all, Burke is a cognitive critic for whom the intellectual form of a literary work and the dramatic form of an idea are the main concern. Burke tries to discover the active principle of an idea, a character, a lyric.

John Crowe Ransom's placing of Burke as a dialectical critic is right, but it is connected with a somewhat misleading distinction. "There are two kinds of poetry (or at least of 'literature') and Burke analyzes one kind with great nicety, and honors it, but shows too little interest in the other. The one he honors is the dialectical or critical kind, and the one he neglects is the lyrical or radical kind."[26] Burke doesn't neglect the lyric: his interest is in its dialectic. Thus Burke reads Keats's "Ode to a Nightingale" as an argument in which spirit is liberated from the "scene" of bodily fever in order to achieve a new "immortal" or "heavenly" scene associated with death, which resolves all the earthly contradictions. Burke's reading is based on biographical speculation about Keats's illness and his love affair with Fanny Brawne, something of a heresy in the world of New Criticism. Burke insists that "linguistic analysis has opened up new possibilities in the correlating of producer and product—and these concerns have an important bearing upon matters of culture and conduct in general that no sheer conventions or ideals of criticism should be allowed to interfere with their development."[27] The analysis can be read as an illustration of the scene/act ratio (an essential feature of dramatism), but it can also be read independently as an illumination of the poem.

As is the case with every Burkean perspective, limited it as it is in one sense, it is all-consuming and totalizing in another. If Burke is the adversary of all forms of reduction and demystification, he nevertheless proves himself to be an obsessive translator (or, as Rorty would put it, redescriber) of forms of thought into his own privileged *dramatistic* vocabulary. Thus other terms that have had powerful explanatory or descriptive functions in other discourses are subsumed under the pentad: for example, idealism under agent, mysticism under purpose, realism under act, pragmatism under agency.[28] This is not reduction, because the intention is not to show the illusoriness of the terms being redescribed, but rather their functional or active roles in the world. Nothing in Burke's system precludes the possibility of translating his pentad into another system for other purposes.

Burke's pragmatic/perspectival approach implies the possibility of other perspectival approaches. Indeed, he encourages "perspective by incongruity," what the Russian formalists called defamiliarization, "by which you deprive yourself of [the] familiarity of a particular perspective in order to see things in a new way."[29] But the question remains: Why should the pentad have the superior or privileged status that it does have in Burke's discourse? Burke's own skepticism about the provisionality of other people's intellectual and imaginative structures would seem to leave him open to Max Black's criticism.

It is perfectly clear that he is *not* faithful to his recommended ironical and compassionate contemplation of the foibles and embarrassments of human thought: it does not take long to find out that "dramatism" is an alias for neo-aristotelianism and that materialists, pragmatists, positivists, and naturalists are going to take a beating for neglecting essential aspects of the mystic pentad. But how is this preference for the five-fold description of human motives grounded?[30]

And yet a case can be made for the intellectual generosity of Burke's dramatism: it is a sort of vehicle of negative capability, which permits him to elicit what is persuasive in a variety of perspectives. Unlike the postmodern perspectivism of Rorty and others, it has an unlimited view, perhaps to the point of naivete, of the possibility of communication among perspectives. In *The Criticism of Culture and the Culture of Criticism,* Giles Gunn rightly stresses the openness of Burke's system or systems, his comic and playful sense of the vulnerability of all essentialist categories, and his willingness to revise and abandon in the light of new situations.[31] Burke's stance is pragmatic, "strategic," ever alive to the instance at hand.

I don't know that a philosophically justifiable ground for Burke's dramatism can be discovered. One may speculate, however, about the reason or reasons for Burke's attraction to dramatism. It is clear from the beginning of his career that, to quote Bewley once again, "poetry [one might emend it to verbal discourse in general] becomes, not a segregated experience, but an experience at one with all human action."[32] Dramatism serves Burke's activist, propagandistic, didactic needs. But it goes beyond propaganda and didactism. Dramatism is a vision of life and its textual embodiment as a contention of character, voices, moods. "We contend that 'perspective by incongruity' makes for a *dramatic* vocabulary, with weighting and counter-weighting, in contrast with the liberal ideal of *neutral* naming in the characterization of process."[33] But the contention avoids mutual destruction through a comic framing, which Burke benignly proclaims to be "most serviceable for the handling of human relationships."[34] The comic view implies an awareness of limitation of each character's claim. It acknowledges the egoistic, materialistic drive in human beings, but it "avoids the . . . dangers of cynical debunking" by promoting a "realistic sense of one's limitations."[35] For all of Burke's eschewing of the liberal idea of neutrality, he is very much attached to the liberal idea of accommodation. Burke's revolutionism is toothless. Burke's dramatism invites comparison with Bakhtin's dialogism, but it is considerably more benign, perhaps a sign of the difference in the historical situations of the two writers.

The ungroundedness of Burke's pentad suggests the permanent tension in his work between the modernist perspectivalist and the nineteenth century totalizer. How does one harmoniously encompass the world while respecting the differences within it, an especially problematic task if the individual perspectives are incongruous and not complementary? The effect of contradiction and incongruity in Burke is to produce a new kind of nonsynthetic writing. Burke's deepest moral and political ambition is to resolve murderous conflict in order to create a kind of global unity in difference. In *Language as Symbolic Action*, Burke describes his development in the following way: "Basically, the situation is this. I began in the aesthete tradition. In *Counter-Statement*, I made a shift from 'self expression' to 'communication,' happiest when I can transform dyad into triad—'consummation.' "[36] The dyad (or what structuralists call binary oppositions) contains positive and negative terms, but Burke is careful to protect the idea of the negative from connotations of evil or inferiority. Triad suggests synthesis: the dialectical totalizing of Hegelian or Marxian thought. Perspective by incongruity suggests a resistance to ultimate reconciliations. I am not sure whether we are in the presence of a fundamental contradiction in Burke's view, or an unresolved tension. Perhaps encompassment is the appropriate word for Burke's intention. He wants to encompass the world without dissolving difference. He wants world government without eliminating nations. The last sentence is not intended as a metaphor, for Burke's speculations have the political ambition of world peace.

The very movement of this exposition shows the impossibility of confining Burke to the role of mere literary critic. His perspective encompasses the world. There remains however an unworldliness in Burke's approach. He cultivates the illusion of linguistic solutions to problems of ideology and power (the approach of semanticists contemporary with him like Stuart Chase). Unlike poststructuralists, who continually stress the insurmountable gulf between word and world, Burke sees the world in the word, although not in the aesthetic sense of depriving the world of its physical, biological, political, and social substance.

In a recent book, *Criticism and Social Change*, Frank Lentricchia uses Burke as a club to beat modernist "theories of aesthetic autonomy"[37] and the "debilitated criticism" of Paul de Man's deconstructionism, the "main effect [of which] is political paralysis."[38] Against the background of the radical skepticism of deconstructive theory, Burke's engagement with the world seems salutary indeed. But the placing of Burke against de Man, the aligning of him with Gramsci is itself an exercise in ahistorical abstraction, a sign of a felt despair about the current state of literary studies rather than a true assessment of Burke's status as an activist thinker and a political theorist. What this latest effort to redeem Burke for contemporary literary politics overlooks is not only the attractive and archaic Aristotelian devotion to rational coherence (to hierarchy and perfection) but also the skepticism that runs counter to all reifications (to use a contemporary jargon word) that make him so interesting a player with ideas. It is no service to Burke's extraordinary achievement to enlist him in causes for which he was not equipped to fight.

CHAPTER SIX

Ideology and Ethical Criticism

In a passage I have already quoted, Marius Bewley says that for Burke "poetry becomes not a segregated experience, but an experience at one with all human action. . . . Poetry is therefore seen to be ethical, and one of the deepest influences in shaping our structures of orientation."[1] What is the relationship between ideology critique and ethical criticism? I would like to address the question in responding to Wayne Booth's recent book, *The Company We Keep: An Ethics of Fiction*. Although Burke and Booth are critics of quite different temperaments, there are important affinities between them. Both have been formed by an Aristotelian poetics. They consider themselves pluralists and share a preoccupation with rhetoric as the medium of ethical expression and action.

Booth begins his book by recalling how during the early 1960s he and his colleagues at the University of Chicago could ignore the distress of a young black assistant professor, Paul Moses, who declared that he would no longer teach *Huckleberry Finn* because he found the portrayal of Jim offensive. Booth remembers with more than a twinge of conscience that he and his colleagues found the challenge to Mark Twain's great novel offensive because it violated "academic norms of objectivity."[2] Anyone teaching literature and writing criticism nowadays knows that the appeal to objectivity will no longer do. Indeed, any such appeal may even be suspected, for instance in the case of the challenge to *Huckleberry Finn,* of masking a racist bias. Booth does not admit a racist bias in the making of academic norms, but he is convinced that the peremptory dismissal of Moses' challenge to a canonical work was profoundly wrong and *The Company We Keep* is in part an attempt to show why.

Booth undertakes to reread *Huckleberry Finn* with the challenge in mind to see what he can learn about the book and about his own ethical assumptions in reading it. In a similar spirit, he engages the feminist challenge to Rabelais' sexism in *Gargantua and Pantagruel,* and to Jane Austen's complicity with male authority in *Emma,* works he has long loved and admired. The reconsiderations of Rabelais, Austen and Twain, however, are only a part of a larger enterprise to rehabilitate what in 1988 appeared to be the nearly lost practice of ethical criticism.

Why did ethical criticism lose authority, so that it had to be rehabilitated? I can only sketch a possible answer to the question. In the modernist aesthetic there has always been a tension between art and morality. The value terms of the New Criticism, irony, paradox and ambiguity, could not be expected to provide a clear guide to conduct. It is not that morality had no role to play in the imagination, but that it had to be disengaged from a moralistic understanding of its role. Thus in "The Art of Fiction" Henry James attacks Walter Besant's phrase "conscious moral purpose" in order to formulate what he believes to be the "point at which the moral and the aesthetic sense lie very near together; that is in the light of the very obvious truth that the deepest quality of a work of art will always be the quality of the mind of the producer."[3] And in the Preface to *The Portrait of A Lady,* James speaks of "the 'moral' sense of a work of art" as dependent "on the amount of felt life conceived in producing it."[4] The morality of a work of art for James is its candor in expressing the truth of that felt life. Moral is enclosed in quotation marks, suggesting an uneasiness about the Victorian tendency to *identify* the moral with the artistic. But that uneasiness does not lead to a divorce between art and the moral sense. James's novels act out the productive tension between art and morality. During the 1940s and 1950s, moral critics like Lionel Trilling and F. R. Leavis, great admirers of James, had immense authority. That authority vanishes with the advent during the 1960s of a more theoretically rigorous criticism. What you have is a "conspiracy" of structuralists (anticipated by Northrop Frye's attempt to put criticism on a scientific basis) and radically skeptical poststructuralists who in effect confine evaluative criticism (ethical and aesthetic) to the capricious history of taste. One might say that structuralists and poststructuralists effectively divorced literature not only from ethical but from aesthetic considerations as well.

In recent years, the ethical has returned sometimes in the guise of political ideology, gender, and race. It is not fortuitous that Booth begins his work with Paul Moses. The challenge to *Huckleberry Finn* during the early 1960s was a harbinger of the revolts during the latter part of the decade, revolts that persist in the academic politics of the 1980s and the 1990s. The ethical has not only returned, it has become inescapable.

The Company We Keep (nine years in the making) appeared at a moment when ethical issues have already established themselves as the matter of renewed literary and philosophical concern. I have in mind the recent work of Hillis Miller (*The Ethics of Reading*), Tobin Sieber (*The Ethics of Criticism*), Alasdair MacIntyre (*After Virtue*), and Barbara Hernnstein Smith (*Contingencies of Value*). (I cite a range of works so different in their intentions and conceptions of the topic that one would be hard put to generalize the ethical from the work of these critics. What is interesting, however, is that they feel compelled at the moment they write to formulate an *ethics* of criticism.) What Booth has rediscovered is that ethical criticism is in a sense a redundancy, since all criticism, whether it knows it or not, is value-laden, even criticism that thinks of itself as value neutral. Booth chooses to call ethical what others might call ideological.

The ideological and the ethical, however, should not be confused. "Ideological" evokes the demystifying aggressiveness of much of the advanced criticism being written now. Ideology, in other words, is concerned with issues of power. For instance, the ideological critic may unmask the moral pretenses of arbitrary power, may reveal the ways in which an ethical language naturalizes structures of oppression, but if he or she is committed, let us say, to a Foucauldian view of the ultimacy of the power motive, then the terrain of criticism becomes simply the power struggle. Ethical criticism assumes the possibility that questions of justice and morality can be addressed in a more or less disinterested way, that there is, at the very least, a tension between (moral) reason and power. However responsive an ethical critic may be to conclusions arrived at by way of ideology, the ethical critic must resist the language of power. (The difference between ethical and ideological critics corresponds to the difference between Socrates and the sophists. Disinterested truth remains a possibility in the Socratic tradition. The sophists, the ideologues of antiquity, deny the distinction between knowledge and opinion in teaching a rhetoric of power.) The ideological critic represents a constituency, usually the dispossessed; the ethical critic speaks for him or herself, the struggle is for the individual soul.

Booth's particular stance, liberal or pluralist as he prefers to call it, is a scrupulously generous effort to respond to the ideological challenges in the ethical style. His strategy is disarming. Booth will very rarely do battle with books (i.e., implied authors) or critics. His metaphor for the world of books is a commonwealth of friends. He approaches each book as offering the prospect of friendship, though its realization may be an arduous critical process. Even a writer like D. H. Lawrence, for whom Booth has always had an instinctive aversion, must be recuperated for the commonwealth. His method is to begin with an indictment: "Can you think of any major novelist, other than Dreiser perhaps, who provides more invitation to stop reading and start complaining about style? . . . But troubles with style are only the beginning. . . . We have by now had generations of novelists and psychologists claiming to save the world through some phallic redemption, . . . but after decades of such talk, after the multiplying sex manuals and *Playboy* philosophisings, it can seem old hat. . . . My resistances extend beyond the sexual nostrums to the whole range of panaceas offered in the *Salvator Mundi*."[5] "The friend replies" by insisting on a rereading of the text (in this case *Women in Love*) in which Lawrence seems to endorse Birkin's megalomaniacal preference of his own madness to sanity. Booth now reproaches himself for having "missed the point."

> Lawrence was experimenting with what it means for a novelist to lose his own distinct voice in the voices of his characters. In the search for an authentic self, any sensitive modern spirit living without love must end either in despair like Ursula's or in a half-mad ecstasy like Birkin's. By dramatizing their conclusions as if they were conclusive, Lawrence tries consciously or unconsciously, to build in us a longing for the only condition that he thinks can save us—a longing for what he elsewhere calls "the Holy Ghost" of self-purged selfhood.

He winds up valuing Lawrence for his "dialogical" responsiveness to the other, his knowledge that "human beings cannot be saved except in loving others" (446, 449). Booth has seen the openness that Lawrence's dogmatic manner often conceals. His conversion is impressive, though I feel the presence of an ulterior motive, the desire for a new friendship.

Even when he decides to submit his cherished books *Gargantua and Pantagruel*, *Huckleberry Finn*, and *Emma* to the test under pressure from the challenges of criticism sensitive to sexism and racism, he allows his new attention to the works to unsettle his relationship, not to destroy but to preserve it on a new basis. He has also befriended the critics in the process. Booth has the least trouble in responding to the criticism that Jane Austen identifies the happiness of her female characters (e.g., Emma) with the world as males constitute it. In an eloquent discussion of Austen's work, he strengthens his relationship to it. He concedes that the conventional form of the novel requires the resolution of a marriage plot with the woman in effect submitting to male authority. But he discovers an "antidote" in the implied author (a concept Booth first formulated in *The Rhetoric of Fiction*), "who provides the subtle clues to Knightley's own egotism. . . . She creates for us the imaginative and witty vitality of Emma herself, as a criticism of the one-sided wisdom and stately power of Knightley" (433). (Booth's effort to redeem Jane Austen will not, of course, satisfy radical feminists or gay and lesbian critics who view the marriage plot as marginalizing behavior that deviates from the ideal of heterosexual monogamy.)

The challenge of Rabelais is more formidable. Booth will no longer simply accept the ideal of sexual equality promoted by the Abbey of Theleme. The concrete evidence of comically endorsed scurrilous treatment of women would seem to support feminist indignation at Rabelais.

> How are we to respond, for example, to the famous episode that almost everyone would consider as in itself sexist, the trick Panurge plays upon the Lady of Paris who refuses his advances? He sprinkles her gown with ground-up pieces of genitals of a bitch in heat and then withdraws to watch the sport, as all the male dogs of Paris assemble to piss on her, head to toe. . . . Her offense, remember, is simply that she turned Panurge down and—I suppose—that she is a woman of high degree. (400, 401)

Booth entertains and rejects Bakhtin's defense of Rabelaisian scatological laughter as a "progressive force, the expression of an ideology that opposes the official and authoritarian languages that dominate our surfaces." He rejects the defense because the laughter in this instance and others is directed not against authoritarian languages but against women. Women and their sexuality are a blind spot in Rabelais writing and for that matter in Bakhtin's as well. Booth entertains various historical defenses, for example, that Rabelais "wrote before anyone . . . had thought more than ten minutes about what equality for women might mean," but he rejects them in the name of the present. "The historical defense scants my responsibility to myself and my living friends" (409, 410). It is not clear why reading cannot be doubleminded, at once historical and contemporary. But Booth's critique has a different, more troubling, implication that I want to consider.

What he says about Rabelais could be said about any funny joke at the expense of women, blacks, Jews, and Poles. He seems troubled by Rabelais's failure to distance himself from Panurge's scandalous behavior, but that strikes me as an irrelevant consideration. Cruel as the joke is, it is funny and by distancing himself, the teller of the joke would only take away from the fun. One should tell the story as it should be told for its full impact or simply not tell it. I know that movements for equality and rights tend to breed a solemnity that lead some to say that such jokes should disappear. Ethical consciousness cannot be an all in all, because it would atrophy, for instance, the sense of comedy, in which cruelty plays a part. Booth knows that ethical consciousness has its limits in the imaginative life. He cites Mark Twain's caution that finding a moral in a tale can destroy a story and he admits that "my ethical criticism has for me weakened some of the comic power of Panurge's prank" (458). It is surprising that Booth, good Aristotelian that he is, did not defend the homeopathic value of comedy, however cruel, in venting feelings that would otherwise be repressed or, worse, express themselves in socially and politically noxious ways. I know of no evidence in psychological or sociological research that suggests that jokes establish or perpetuate social and political practices that are dangerously racist or sexist.

In defending the *cathartic* cruelty of humor, I may be recuperating the cruelty for ethical criticism, in effect saying that it is good for the psyche to be able to laugh aggressively without inhibitions and good for society to be able to discharge vicious feelings in the safety of laughter. It may be the case that certain groups in society have suffered so terribly and continue to be so vulnerable that no joke, however funny, can deflect the cruelty. The fact is that ethnic and racial groups often enjoy a cruel humor at their own expense. Indeed, some of the most vicious self-directed humor is generated by the groups themselves. It is a mark of ethnic or racial confidence that the object of humor becomes complicit in the enjoyment of it. Booth may be conceding too much too soon.

What about the immoralities of racism or sexism that are not necessarily funny? The problems even with *Huckleberry Finn* do not essentially involve comedy. There are also instances that Booth does not address (*The Merchant of Venice*, Pound's *Cantos*, the list could be very long). One might defend ethically noxious artistic representations in the interests of the imagination. V. S. Naipaul writes admiringly of Trollope's prejudices (his hatred of Baptists and the cruelty of his humor) not because they are morally justifiable, but because they belong to his imaginative energy and clarity. Naipaul, of course, is revealing himself in this judgment.

Ethical criticism does not necessarily resolve issues of interpretation and aesthetic criticism. It complicates the reading, divides the reader against himself, creates tension. Now convinced of "Twain's full indifference" to Jim's plight, the occasion of fun and games for Huck and Tom Sawyer, and to "the full meaning of slavery and emancipation," Booth experiences "a distressing disparity between the force of my objections . . . and the strength of my continuing love for the book" (477). He continues to value Twain's "preeminent *comic* genius," his "provid[ing] me with a kind of moral holiday while stimulating my thoughts about moral issues" (475).

But Booth is not truly distressed, for he immediately appropriates the distress to his pluralist vision of "imaginative worlds . . . constituted of manifold values that can never be fully realized in any one work or any one critic's endeavor" (477). Booth here reminds one of Bakhtin, whose work represents a continual equivocation between a model of conflict and one of dialogue in which the conflict is almost always accommodated to a benign outcome. Like Burke, Booth is almost always on the side of accommodation. Above all, he wants to hear the voice of the other, to allow the adversary to speak and even to make a friend of him. He does nothing to jeopardize his friendships with both Paul Moses and Mark Twain.

Pluralism does not have a good press these days, a surprising fact in the light of the "authoritative" claims of recent self-described neopragmatic, antifoundationalist critics that all truth-claims are subjectively determined and we have no way of establishing the *objective* superiority of any particular perspective. The reason is that perspectivism has become a doctrine justifying insurgencies, particularly of blacks and women, against established cultural and political authority. Pluralism has come to be associated with a vapid, undiscriminating hospitality to all points of view, so that the repressed voice demanding its right to be heard may be drowned in sheer multiplicity. Booth's version of pluralism is a pluralism with limits, which he vigorously demonstrates in close discriminating readings of texts. But his tone never becomes shrill with indignation. He wants to do right by books and the world, but he is not an agent for transforming the world.

Pluralism in *The Company We Keep* is a multiple role-playing self, always available to new possibilities of experience and self-realization. In affirming the proliferation of the self, Booth does not fear the loss of integrity, because I think he is implicitly committed to an Aristotelian idea of potentiality. Roles are not gratuitously bestowed: they reflect a strategy of "building a richer character." Our virtues "are originally gained by practices that our enemies might call faking, our friends perhaps something like aspiring or emulating." Booth wittily calls this moral process "an hypocrisy upward" (253, 254). It is a stroke of genuine imagination for him to have appropriated contemporary "discourse" of inauthenticity for the ethical criticism. Thus he can dissociate himself from the sentiment of Nathan Zuckerman, the novelist hero of Philip Roth's *The Counterlife*, who declares himself at once a complete role player and a nonentity. "All I can tell you with certainty is that I, for one, have no self. . . . What I have instead is a variety of impersonations I can do, and not only of myself—a troupe of players that I have internalized, a company of actors. . . . I am a theater and nothing more than a theater." Booth responds by saying "to me it doesn't quite feel that way" (259). He apparently experiences the quiddity of his own being, for which he may not, however, be able to give a satisfactory theoretical account.

If the self exists independently of its theatrical impersonations, it is, according to Booth, a multiple, not a unitary self. Moreover, its multiplicity exceeds any imaginative representation of it.

> But readers who engage in a story, readers who enter the pattern of hopes, fears, and expectations that every story asks for, will always take on "characters" that are superior, on the scale of a book's fixed norms, to the relatively complex, erratic and paradoxical characters that they cannot help being in their daily lives. To engage sympathetically with a story is always to concentrate one's actual confusing multi-dimensionality into a small range of values. (255)

This goes counter not only to Roth's conception of the self as a theater but also to Milan Kundera's more plausible account of the relationship between art and life. "I have known all these situations [in *The Unbearable Lightness of Being*], I have experienced them myself, yet none of them has given rise to the person my curriculum vitae and I represent. The characters in my novels are my own unrealized possibilities."[6]

The lucidity of Booth's plain speech reveals his desire to persuade rather than to intimidate. Where ideological critics or self-described critics of ideologies make enemies, Booth is devoted to making friends. In a time of ideological conflict it is a salutary act of self-definition for a critic to present himself in the role of friend.

Booth's generosity of spirit distinguishes him from the very critics whose challenges he has taken so seriously.

But I must confess to having reservations about the way friendship develops in *The Company We Keep*. When Booth wrote his book, the phrase "political correctness" had not achieved its present currency. It is clear in retrospect, however, that he was already responding to the phenomenon ambivalently: that is to say, defensively and concessively. The question then becomes how much Booth's generosity of spirit is compromised by an anxiety not to offend. In fairness to Booth, it should be acknowledged immediately that this anxiety is widespread. It is an affliction in the academy, and I confess to my share in it. But for that reason, it needs to be confronted. Should we assign to this anxiety the term "ethical"? I think not, for if the ethical is a mark of freedom, choice and agency, it should be free of the determinism of the anxiety to please or to have a friend. Earlier I distinguished between the ethical and the ideological as involving a distinction between individual conscience and group consciousness. I would add a distinction between freedom and determinism. The ethical critic acts as if he is free to choose and decide on his or her own; the ideological critic is determined in his choices by the interests of his constituency. The distinctions I am making lie athwart the distinctions Booth makes. As I understand him, he has pretty much conflated the ethical and the ideological and opposed them both to the aesthetic, which permits a morally irresponsible response to the pleasures of the text ("a kind of moral holiday"). It may seem perverse of me to suggest that at this time when ideology reigns and assumes an ethical guise that the aesthetic response may itself be a manifestation of the ethical. When Booth speaks of the "strength of his continuing love for" *The Adventures of Huckleberry Finn*, despite the force of his objections (influenced by his ideological friends), it is at least a question where the ethical lies—with his love or with his objections.

CHAPTER SEVEN

Freud on Trial

I am aware that my own charge against ideology critique is itself an exercise in ideology critique. Am I caught in a familiar contradiction of undermining the validity of what I am asserting by the validity of what I am doing? If I am right, am I then not wrong? This would be the case only if I were rejecting ideology critique as an activity per se and not as a global activity. The only way out of the infinite regress of self-contradiction is to assert, as I do, that there are more things in the world than are dreamed of by ideology.

Ideology critique is a valuable activity. My criticism is directed toward its hubristic ambition. The question then becomes: how does one limit the role of demystification? How does one decide which appearances are to be mistrusted? Intuition, wisdom, experience would seem to be the best guides—perhaps the only guides. They may not be absolutely reliable, but they are guides that we use in the ordinary conduct of our lives with more or less success. Never to suspect is to be naive, always to suspect paranoiac. But this answer does not really help us out in matters of theory.

Certain theories depend on a method of unmasking or of inverting meanings: for instance, psychoanalysis with its *systematic* distinction between manifest and latent content. To want to impose limits on the method, because of a general mistrust of the habit of unmasking might create insuperable difficulties for the development of the theory. (It would be arbitrary to allow certain theories like Freudian theory unmasking privileges while disallowing those privileges to other theories like Marxian theory because of political or moral predilections in favor of the conclusions of one theory over the other.) Perhaps what is needed are self-imposed limits to the jurisdiction of a theory, for instance of the kind Freud imposes in his interpretation of *Oedipus Rex* and *Hamlet*, when he says that he is engaged in hyperinterpretation (at a level below the level of literary interpretation) and disavows the desire to preempt moral or aesthetic perspectives. But it would be misleading to suggest that Freudian theory does not escape the objections that I have leveled against the ideology critics.

There is an interesting paradox in Freud's current status. He is one of the great modern demystifiers whose work and character are the object of a fierce revisionist demystification. Revisionist scholarship on Freud has become a total assault on his scientific claims, his clinical practice and his moral integrity. If it were to succeed, virtually nothing would be left to value in his work. What would remain is a view of his legacy as a poison in our culture that needs to be purged. Two recent publishing events show how far the anti-Freud attack has carried, a featured review of four works of revisionist literature by Frederick Crews in the highbrow *New York Review of Books* and a cover story in the middlebrow *Time* that raises the question "Is Freud Dead?"[1] Crews himself was once a distinguished practitioner of psychoanalytic criticism. The ferocity of his attack has all the animus of a resentful renegade. Freud, the riddle-solver, identified himself with Oedipus. In the eyes of Crews and others, he has become Laius, an invitation to parricide.[2]

Crews devotes a good deal of space to Freud's alleged unscrupulousness in the cooking of evidence (e.g., his unreliable reporting of what actually occurred in his therapeutic encounters), and in his manipulation of patients to serve the interests of psychoanalysis. He recounts a story of how Freud induced a patient and protégé to divorce his wife and marry one of his own patients, a bank heiress, who would then provide funds for Freud's psychoanalytic projects. Freud was able to accomplish this feat by persuading the protégé that he was a latent homosexual and that the new marriage would somehow keep him from a homosexual fate. "The divorce and remarriage" resulted "in the deaths of both of the abandoned, devastated spouses," an early suit for divorce by the newly married woman and repeated attempts at suicide by Freud's protégé.[3]

But this is mere gossip compared to the charge that the seduction theory, central to psychoanalysis, was an invention of Freud's without much basis in clinical experience—that he induced his patients to believe in events they did not remember before they came for analysis. Having then decided that these events did not actually take place, Freud concluded that they were fantasies of the patients, in effect erasing their origins in his own theory. His critics lay recent scandals in repressed memory therapy and clinical practice at the door of his own theory and practice. What emerges is a view of psychoanalytic theory as an imaginative construction drawn from Freud's own fantasy life and a clinical enterprise cynically devoted to supporting it at all costs.

Should Freud's character be an issue in the controversy about Freud's achievement? Character is an issue, it seems to me, when the matter under consideration is Freud's work as a practicing psychoanalyst. If the charges leveled at him are true, they must inevitably affect our judgment of him as a clinician. But their relevance to his work as a theorist is another matter. Unless it can be shown that malfeasance in clinical work communicated to his theoretical formulations, Freud's character flaws, whatever they may be, have no place in the discussion. Crews, basing himself in part on the work of Jeffrey Masson, argues that the vicissitudes of Freud's seduction theory reflect personal corruption. Whether or not one agrees with him, Crews's concern with Freud's character is relevant in this connection. But there is an insinuation that permeates the argument that all of Freud's work is infected by his deplorable character. Since Freudian theory is not a single theory, but rather a rich and heterogeneous body of speculation, it is incumbent upon the critic to show where the issue of character is pertinent and where it is not. Our literary, philosophical, scientific, and artistic traditions would collapse under the weight of the deplorable characters who created them if character automatically became an issue. In fairness to the revisionist critics, however, one should point out that the question of character does not originate with them. Freud's character has been the subject of hagiography and has contributed to the depiction of Freud's monumental achievement by his admirers.

The main thrust of the attack on Freud is that he lacks scientific credibility. Anyone who tries to understand the issues finds himself on treacherous ground. There is first the question of whether Freud's status as a thinker depends on his claim as a scientist. The philosopher of science Adolf Grünbaum takes Freud at his word that he be judged as a scientist and finds him wanting. Jürgen Habermas and Paul Ricoeur reject Freud's "scientistic self-misunderstanding" and claim him for hermeneutics. Grünbaum and Karl Popper, both severe critics of Freud, disagree about whether Freud's thought is falsifiable (a necessary condition of science). Grünbaum argues that it is, Popper that it is not. Who is right— Grünbaum or Popper? It is not an easy question to answer. There are surely claims by Freud that are susceptible to falsification. Grünbaum's obsessive example is the relation between paranoia and repressed homosexuality. He asserts that the evidence shows that Freud was wrong in declaring that paranoia is caused by repressed homosexuality. (I am not so sure that paranoia and repressed homosexuality are the determinate "quantities" that

Grünbaum assumes, indeed must assume if falsifiability is possible.) Even if one can agree on what might constitute falsifiable claims, a vast body of Freud's writing is clearly not susceptible to falsification like the view in *Civilization and Its Discontents* that Eros and Thanatos are equally immortal adversaries, or even the shifting argument in *The Ego and the Id* about the extent to which the ego is submerged in the unconscious. Freudian theory is too protean and multiple for one to be able to say the theory is falsifiable or not.

Moreover, philosophers of science do not hold that scientific theories necessarily rise or fall when statements within the theories are falsified. Theoretical survival depends on the character and degree of falsification. The issue is further complicated if one takes seriously Thomas Kuhn's theory of paradigms in which the demarcation between science and nonscience loses its sharpness. Or even if one does not accept Kuhn's theory of paradigms with its emphasis on contingent historical and subjective factors, one needs to keep in mind that the conception of science itself has a history. (The idea of science as falsifiable is of recent provenance.) And one might ask what would constitute a science of psychology. Do the same standards that hold for physics apply to psychology and if they do, how adequate could a science of psychology be, given the nature of the phenomena involved? Crews's all-out assault takes none of these matters into consideration.

Crews is a formidable polemicist, but "The Unknown Freud" must be judged as an exercise in overkill. The title itself is misleading, as it implies that there is another Freud to be distinguished from the known Freud. What Crews seems to be saying is that the dark, demonic, and criminal Freud that he is describing is the real Freud. There is no other Freud. An unresisting reader of the essay may be impressed, even overwhelmed by the amount of evidence and the polemical energy with which it is deployed. But the energy may arouse suspicion about whether Crews is a careful reporter even of the findings of the revisionist scholars whom he adduces as support for his views. Crews writes with the assurance that only a fool would doubt his claims.

The letters that followed Crews's essay increased the doubts about his reliability. Grünbaum wrote in to dissociate himself from the spirit of the attack. I can offer one telling instance of unreliability in Crews's scholarship. Close to the beginning of the essay, he cites the work of Grünbaum and that of another scholar, Malcolm Macmillan. According to Crews, Grünbaum demonstrates in *Foundations of Psychoanalysis* that "clinical validation" of Freudian hypotheses is an epistemic sieve, that "psychoanalysis is fatally contaminated by the inclusion, among its working assumptions and its dialogue with patients, of the very ideas that supposedly get corroborated by clinical experience" and that "even if Freud's means of gathering evidence had been sound, that evidence couldn't have reliably yielded the usual constructions he placed on it."[4] Crews says that "we cannot be surprised, then, by Malcolm Macmillan's recent exhaustive demonstration that Freud's theories of personality and neurosis—derived as they were from misleading precedents, vacuous pseudophysical metaphors, and a long concatenation of mistaken inferences that *couldn't be subjected to empirical review*—amount to castles in the air [emphasis added]." The footnote to this passage reads: See Adolf Grünbaum, *The Foundations of Psychoanalysis*, etc., and Malcolm Macmillan *Freud Evaluated*. The effect on the exposition and footnote is to illicitly associate Adolf Grünbaum's view with that of Macmillan. Illicitly, because Grünbaum does not believe that Freud's constructions are "castles in the air." Severe as he is with Freud, he takes him very seriously; he believes that Freud's work can be subject to empirical review. It is precisely Grünbaum's task, as he conceives it, to test Freud's work empirically. It is Popper, not Grünbaum, who says that Freud's propositions cannot be falsified.

What are the reasons for the wholesale condemnation of Freud's achievement? The *Time* article suggests several reasons; including the problematical proliferation of "accusations of sexual abuse" based on the recovery of repressed memory, the superior success of drug treatment "in the alleviation of mental disorders," the discovery of numerous "errors, duplicities and fudged evidence" in psychoanalytic studies. These are plausible reasons, but they do not explain the extremity of the attack on Freud, which reflects, I believe, his unusual authority in our culture.

The history of culture is filled with authority figures: Plato, Aristotle, the Church Fathers, thinkers who have guided, if not determined our thinking. Certain writers become objects of idolatry. Their achievements are measured not by their capacity to answer to a reality external to them. They themselves are the measures of truth. Michel Foucault calls them founders of discursivity (Freud and Marx are his examples). They provide the master texts that determine truth-claims. Unlike scientists, these founders of discursivity are not required to conform to the canons of science. Their own discourse constitutes the canon that determines its truth value. "One defines a proposition's theoretical validity in relation to the work of the founders—while, in the case of Galileo and Newton, it is in relation to what physics or cosmology *is* (in its intrinsic structure and 'normativity') that one affirms the validity of any proposition that those men may have put forth. To phrase it very schematically: the voice of initiators of discursivity is not situated in the space that science defines."[5]

Foucault suggests that the modern founders of discursivity are sui generis, but his characterization of them and their followers evokes an older scholastic tradition in which quarrels about doctrinal issues in matters of religious belief were adjudicated by an appeal to the church fathers. Freud and Marx would have both found this comparison with scholasticism odious, since they considered themselves scientists; they would have declared their affinities with Newton and Galileo. But Foucault is nevertheless right in his sense of how Freud has played in modern culture—that is, in his characterization of Freudianism rather than Freud.

Freud and Marx have been the idols of our secular culture so we should not be surprised that they provoke iconoclasm especially in disillusioned idolaters. Crews enacts the role of idol smasher. There is of course an alternative to idolatry on the one hand and iconoclasm on the other: the demotion of the idol to a body of knowledge or knowledge claims, which we may both consult and criticize. We do not need to destroy Marx and Freud, we need only place them with thinkers like Weber and Durkheim, for example, whose texts for all their authority and power are not the final court of appeal. A persuasive criticism of Freud's work must acknowledge its power. He has been read by educated readers who do not or cannot read science—that is, who do not follow the rules of testing truth claims that scientists are supposed to follow. Freud has entered so deeply into our cultural life that his thought has affected even those who have not read him. It does not of course follow from this fact that his influence has been benign. But an attack that simply tries to dispose of Freud's credibility as a scientist has not accounted for his persuasiveness.

We read Freud's work for its heuristic rather than probative value. Grünbaum himself makes this distinction, acknowledging Freud's heuristic power, while asserting the inadequacy of validation in the clinical studies. Indeed, it would be hard to understand why Grünbaum would devote so much of his career to the testing and challenging of Freud's work, if it weren't for its extraordinary suggestiveness. Heuristics is the domain of speculative theory, about whose truth value we may not be certain. Speculative theory is the space of potential truths as yet unproven, perhaps even insusceptible of proof. Imagine the impoverishment of our intellectual life, if the intellect felt constrained from uttering what it could not prove scientifically.

Of course, the argument that speculation *might* be true is weak. The case for Freud can hardly rest on it. If Freud's propositions do not or cannot satisfy the canons of scientific verification, they must satisfy some other standard or expectation to become persuasive. This standard, which Freud provides, is connected with the power of narration. In Freud, narrative and theoretical argument are sometimes indistinguishable. A notable example is his exposition of the Oedipus complex in *The Interpretation of Dreams*. Freud finds his theory, so to speak, in stories, for example, the basic structure of the Oedipus complex in the narrative structure of the Greek legend.

The Oedipus complex is the psychological inhibition of the acted-out narrative of Oedipus's murder of his father and marriage to his mother. In *The Interpretation of Dreams* Freud goes back to the legend of King Oedipus and tells it as the story of all males, who are "destined to direct [their] first sexual impulses toward [their] mothers, and [their] first impulses of hatred and violence toward [their] fathers."[6] He notes that the action of Sophocles's play "consists simply in the disclosure, approached step-by-step, and artistically delayed (. . . comparable to the work of psychoanalysis)" (307). Freud's own interpretation is artistically delayed, withholding until the end the piece of evidence within the Sophoclean text that apparently reveals a proleptic awareness of the Freudian discovery.

> In the very text of Sophocles' tragedy, there is an unmistakable reference to the fact that the Oedipus legend had its source in dream-material of immemorial antiquity, the content of which was the painful disturbance of the child's relations to its parents caused by the first impulses of sexuality. Jocasta comforts Oedipus. . . . "For many a man hath seen himself in dreams his mother's mate, but he who gives no heed to suchlike matters bears the easier life." The dream of having sexual intercourse with one's mother was as common then as it is today with many people, who tell it with indignation and astonishment. As may well be imagined, it is the key to the tragedy and the complement to the dream of the death of the father. (309)

Freud acknowledges that the story can be understood as a conflict between "the all powerful will of the gods and the vain efforts of human beings threatened with human disaster"(307). The moral of this version of the story is "resignation to the divine will." Freud's narrative gives us both his version of the Oedipus story and the Sophoclean version by explaining the play as a displacement from family drama to the theology. Jocasta's speech not only reveals an awareness of the Oedipal drama, it is also a counsel of repression in consciousness, exactly what Freud wishes to overcome. From a

Freudian point of view, the paradox of Sophocles' play is that it at once acts out the Oedipal drama and represses or sublimates it in a story of theological conflict between will and fate. Freud is careful to note that he is not preempting the role of literary critic, but rather engaging in an exercise of hyperinterpretation—which in this case means locating the source of the emotional impact he claims the play has on the reader. Hyperinterpretation in this sense is a kind of demystification.

How does Freud "prove" his theory? Not as a scientist who presents the evidence of experiments and statistical information, but as a storyteller. His criterion for the truth of the Oedipus complex is its persuasive emotional power, its capacity to stir a response in the audience. "If the *Oedipus Rex* is capable of moving a modern reader or playgoer no less powerfully than it moved the contemporary Greeks, the only possible explanation is that the effect of the Greek tragedy does not depend on the conflict between fate and human will, but on the peculiar nature of the material by which this conflict is revealed" (305). We are moved to accept the truth of the Oedipus complex in the way we are moved by the tragedy of *Oedipus Rex*. The criterion is much the same as the one that determines truth in a psychoanalysis: the emotional recognition of the truth of an interpretation. It is, need I add, what determines the reader's or listener's sense of truth in narrative. This authority of emotional response, common to psychoanalytic theory and practice and to narrative, is different from the authority of the truth-claims in science, which have nothing to do with their emotionally persuasive power.

But Freud doesn't say that the ancient Greek audience was not moved by the conflict between fate and human will, so perhaps he should not be so confident in his universalizing claim that the tragic effect does not depend on their (or our) recognition of this conflict. Nor does he provide evidence that it is the incestuous material that stirs the audience (the whole audience? a portion of it? both men and women?). Moreover, persuasiveness is no guarantee of truth, since myths can at the same time persuade and deceive.

I am not sure that skepticism of this kind can ever be overcome. Freud provokes it because his narrative is in the service of a claim to science. But such skepticism would seem captious if it were applied to the great masters of modern literature, who tell comparable stories. Readers are moved by their narratives and testify to a sense of their truth.

Freud's achievement occurs in the company of the great masters of modern literature: Conrad, Lawrence, Mann, and Proust. He is the theoretical formulator of ideas that are discursively or dramatically present in the work of these writers. It is not simply a matter of influence. Conrad was not influenced by Freud in his writing of *Heart of Darkness*. In fact, he had little regard for Freud's work. Lawrence began writing *Sons and Lovers* before he knew anything of Freud and only heightened the Oedipal pattern already in his work after he learned about Freud. Subsequently, he became a critic of Freud's theory. Mann of course was an admirer. What matters is not that Freud influenced or was influenced by these writers, but that they seemed to have arrived at Freud's insights independently.

Most psychoanalytic literary critics use Freudian ideas as a master text to interpret other texts, provoking suspicions among the unconverted that a model of interpretation is being arbitrarily and coercively imposed, much like the psychoanalyst's imposition of his understanding on the experience of patients. And the literary critic is more culpable than the psychoanalyst because the literary critic does not have the excuse of dealing with a living patient who can at least resist an interpretation. The more fruitful and persuasive "use" of Freud is what Peter Brooks does, for example, in placing *Beyond The Pleasure Principle* alongside other modern narratives.[7]

The moderns may not have discovered repression, but they display an exacerbated consciousness of it in the wake of what is experienced as its long Victorian history. The whole panoply of Freudian concepts: the Oedipal drama in the family romance, the degraded split sexuality which results in impotence, the return of the repressed, and so on, are confirmed in the imaginative literature of the modern period. "Confirmation" in this sense is not scientific proof. If repression is the central fact of modern civilization, perhaps its very definition, then the work of literature in its most serious and ambitious version is to reveal the truth of what is repressed. Freud "theorizes" what may be the critical insight of modern literature. His theory can be construed as a narrative of the manifold sublimations of unconscious life in the thoughts, dreams, and behavior of persons.

II

But a defense of Freud cannot confine him to modern literature. He is the inaugurator of the secular confession, which provides human beings the chance to come to an understanding of their unconscious drives. There is an irony in the fact that Freud saw himself in an Enlightenment tradition as a demystifier of religion; he exposes religion as an illusion, an opiate as Marx had done before him. To the extent that the demystification succeeds, it leaves a spiritual or psychic vacuum for the disbeliever. Psychoanalysis in a sense fills the vacuum. Like religion, psychoanalysis is the site of the most intimate portion of a person's life.

In his role as therapist or secular priest, questions about Freud's moral as well as epistemological authority arise. As a narrator of the repressions and sublimations of individual lives and the collective life of civilization, Freud is obliged to sort out self-betraying and defeating lies against the truth of unconscious life and the necessary illusions that protect us against its destructive impact. Freud speaks of the "tact and restraint" necessary to a psychoanalyst "whenever in the course of his work he goes beyond the standard lines of interpretation, [for] his listeners or readers will only follow him as far as their own familiarity with analytic technique will allow them." He urges the analyst "to guard against the risk that an increased display of acumen on his part may be accompanied by a diminution in the certainty and trustworthiness of his results."[8] What is required is a balance of caution and boldness. Freud here seems to be addressing both the psychoanalytic theorist who must convince his readers of the truth of his theory and the psychoanalyst who needs to elicit assent to his interpretations from his patients. It is not altogether clear whether Freud means to give advice about rhetorical strategy and tactics or whether he is expressing the self-doubt that accompanies the formulation of new theory and interpretation. Perhaps he is doing both at once. The evolution of Freud's theory shows him to be fully aware that his ideas are always susceptible to falsification. "It remains for the future to decide whether there is more delusion in my theory than I should like to admit,"[9] he remarks apropos of his case history of the psychotic Doctor Schreber. But it would be wrong to conclude from Freud's cautionary remarks that he solves the problem of authority in the psychoanalytic situation. Unlike contemporaries who wrote fiction, Freud never adopted the position of epistemological relativism. "Point of view" is never his problem. He acknowledged the fact that his own knowledge of unconscious life was incomplete and that psychoanalysts were always in the process of learning more about their patients, but the unchallenged assumption of the relationship between analyst and analysand is the reliability of the knowledge of the analyst and the unreliability of that of the analysand, whose epistemological condition is one of false consciousness.

Like Marx, Freud has been read as a critic of false consciousness, a demystifier of self-defeating illusions. Both thinkers write as if they are in possession of a truth unavailable to others and as if resistance to that truth is paradoxically a confirmation of it. Resistance, according to this view, reflects an unconscious experience of the truth as a threat. In "Dora: An Analysis of a Case of Hysteria," Freud succinctly formulates the principle that resistance confirms the truth of what is being denied.

> My expectations were by no means disappointed when this explanation of mine was met by Dora with a most emphatic negative. The "No" uttered by a patient after a repressed thought has been pre-

sented to his conscious perception for the first time does no more than register the existence of a repression and its severity; it acts, as it were as a gauge of the repression's strength. If this "No," instead of being regarded as the expression of an impartial judgment (of which, indeed, the patient is incapable), is ignored, and if work is continued, the first evidence soon begins to appear that in such a case "No" signifies the desired "Yes."[10]

Freud makes his case through a sleight of phrasing: "the 'No' uttered by a patient after a repressed thought has been presented" excludes the possibility that a "No" has been uttered without a repressed thought. It is reasonable to assume that if a repressed thought has been presented to consciousness that the "No" reflects resistance to it. But for Freud a "No" unrelated to repression is a (theoretical?) impossibility. Because the patient is always the victim of repression, he or she is incapable of impartial judgment. The implication is that neurosis infects the whole person. Freud does not have to demonstrate in each particular instance that a "No" is really a "Yes" by examining the evidence and offering criteria for judgment.[11] It is not hard to see the moral objection to such a view. In its systematic and imperial version, the demystification can never be wrong, which makes it a tyrannical exercise. In its weaker version, resistance may (or may not) be a confirmation of the truth that is being resisted. Marxism too shows little tolerance for those who resist its ideological interpretations: resistance reflects the class attitudes it is determined to demystify. It is characteristic of theories devoted to demystification to reduce all resistance to them to the status of mystification.

Freud betrays his own commitment to the strong view in the metaphor he employs to describe what is required for the analyst to overcome the analysand's resistance.

The length of the road over which an analysis must travel with the patient, and the quantity of material which must be mastered on the way, are of no importance in comparison with the resistance which is met with in the course of the work, and are only of importance at all insofar as they are necessarily proportional to the resistance. The situation is the same as when today an enemy army needs weeks and months to make its way across a stretch of country which in times of peace was traversed by an express train in a few hours and which only a short time before had been passed over by the defending army in a few days.[12]

This is the language of power, not reason. Resistance, Freud seems to say, is always an irrational function, not susceptible to rational persuasion. Psychoanalytic interpretation is not an exercise in reasoning with a person, but rather a battle in which the analyst opportunistically seizes on his adversary's vulnerabilities.

Rationalization, the counterpart to ideology in psychoanalytic theory, is to be demystified through psychoanalysis. What relation does the analysis have to reason? The analyst doesn't persuade the analysand through logic and evidence, but through the artful management of associations the analysand makes of his memories, fantasies, thoughts, and so forth. The management of these associations is based on a theory, presumably the work of reason, that claims access to reality, which rationalization distorts. Like Marx, Freud fails to provide an adequate account of how his theory becomes exempt from the distorting mechanism of rationalization. This is not to say that such an account is not possible. It would have to avail itself of the Kantian conception of the rational faculty as self-critical, the basis for the conception of disinterestedness I put forward in chapter 3. Rationality (as opposed to rationalization) reflects a capacity to think against oneself. This means that the theory must contain within itself a self-doubting habit, not to be confused with the disarming mechanisms of rationalization, which immunize the rationalizer from criticism. Any extensive reading of Freud's work shows him to have this capacity for self-criticism, but it is flawed by defensive investments in his theory and his clinical practice. (Freud is hardly alone in history of thought in this respect!) His failure to credit the analysand with any rational authority brings to mind the arrogance of the ideology critic who learns about the text, but has learned nothing from it.

Perhaps nothing provokes more resistance to Freud than the doctrine of resistance. Psychoanalysis assumes that the person does not know his own interests and needs to be brought to an awareness of them through the instrumentality of a knowing agent (the psychoanalyst). The potentiality for coerciveness is always present when the powers of self-awareness are delegated to someone else. Ideally, the psychoanalyst is no more than a catalyst who makes the reaction possible without entering into or distorting it. But the case histories of Freud and others tell us otherwise and the reason is simple: an analyst is a human being with all the limitations and distortions of his finitude, which can never be fully neutralized. The potentiality for tyranny lies in the asymmetry of authority between analyst and analysand. Lacan tried to equalize the relationship by reinventing the figure of the analyst as a suffering human being. But it is difficult to see how this solves the problem of authority since the suffering analyst in his specialized knowledge still claims access to the truth of which the analysand is ignorant. Of course, the problem of the asymmetry of human relationships is pervasive in human life: between parents and children, between husbands and wives, between lovers, and even between friends. The problem is exacerbated, however, when the asymmetry is institutionalized and sanctioned.

For the most part, modern writers do not share Freud's confidence. They may unmask the deceptions and self-deceptions of characters, but they are uncertain about what exists underneath. John Dowell, Ford Madox Ford's narrator, repeatedly testifies to his ignorance of character (including his own) in *The Good Soldier*. The truth of character is indeterminate. The conception of the unconscious as inchoate and ultimately unfathomable might have led Freud to a similar view: sometimes he even seems to hold it. But as the hero-narrator of his case histories, he assumes the privilege of certain knowledge that distinguishes him from most of his modern contemporaries. Freud's confidence derives from a role that he unconsciously played (and which every psychoanalyst inevitably performs): that of a priest, a confessor to the secular-minded, to those without religion who nevertheless require its benefits. One might imagine Freud's emphatic "No" to this interpretation, given his view of religion as an illusion, but the need to be heard, judged, and consoled by a wise spiritually endowed person may be incorrigible.

In a time of epistemological skepticism and democratic suspicion of authority, Freud's confidence in his own intellectual and moral authority is bound to be suspect. The suspicion is only exacerbated by alleged instances of Freud's reprehensible conduct in his professional and personal life. But the problem of authority in Freud reflects a confusion about the status of his thought. Interpretation is not scientific explanation, and it always implies the possibility of competing interpretations. Freud's great contribution to psychology was in establishing and enriching the interpretive mode in its attempt to discover the hidden motives of thoughts, dreams, behavior. Psychoanalysis then, like literary criticism, may be a fruitful conflict of interpretations. Freud and his followers are most vulnerable, it would seem, when they attribute to a particular interpretation, rather than the activity of interpretation itself, an authority it has not earned. Moreover, one can quarrel with the interpretive mode as an exclusive means of understanding personality, thoughts, feelings, behavior, because of its unwillingness to accept anything in its own terms, on its face value. Interpretation implicitly confers authority on the interpreter at the expense of the interpreted. It involves translation or reduction or demystification.

Grünbaum, the most formidable critic of Freud's scientific pretensions, insists that Freud stands or falls as a scientist. Since Freudian theory is a theory of causation, all attempts to transform it into hermeneutics represents an illicit attempt to evade the responsibility of empirical verification. It is an evasion, it seems to me, only if one continues to insist on Freud's status as a scientist. The effect of such an insistence is to deprive us of a vast body of insight and intellectual provocation. If Freudian theory is neither a science nor interpretation, it is nothing. By redescribing Freud's theory in hermeneutic terms, one is engaged in a saving operation.

Against Grünbaum one can invoke Wittgenstein who had similar objections to Freud's theory and yet was fascinated not by "its supposed kinship with science, but [by] its completely unprecedented character as an art of interpretation, invented and practiced by Freud with an impressive (and at the same time slightly unnerving) virtuosity."[13] (The difference between Crews and Grünbaum is that Crews has decided that Freud is for the most part worthless or pernicious, whereas Grünbaum only claims that Freud's theory is for the most part not proven. Unlike Crews, Grünbaum has not closed the case against Freud.) Whereas the effect of Grünbaum's reading of Freud (and that of Crews who follows him) is to demystify his scientific claims, to show him to be in error, the effect of recasting Freud as an interpreter is to remove from an evaluation of his work draconian standards of right and wrong, illusion and reality. The question becomes not whether Freud's theory is the right one (and other theories wrong), but that of its cogency and persuasiveness in the realm of hermeneutics, which accommodates a heterogeneity of interpretation. The justification for changing the ground in our understanding of Freud is well expressed in Jacques Bouveresse's discussion of Wittgenstein's reading of Freud. "What is not so clear is how [Wittgenstein] might determine whether a scientific treatment of the phenomena concerned is possible and under what conditions, or whether, as some would have it, psychoanalysis may not be scientific but nonetheless constitutes the most scientific, or at any rate the most convincing thing we have, given the nature of the phenomena in question."[14]

In endorsing the redescription of Freud's theory as one of interpretation, I am rejecting the view of his idolaters, who persist in taking Freud at his word when he describes himself as a scientist who offered his theory as a scientific theory of causation. The question then becomes, If the theory cannot be empirically verified, or if obversely, it can be falsified, does that demolish it or can it be redescribed in a way that will preserve its explanatory powers? My own view is that the view of psychoanalysis as interpretive enterprise does not entail the complete abandonment of a causal idiom in characterizing behavior, thought and fantasy. It does entail greater modesty and uncertainty in one's knowledge claims: the kind of modesty we exercise in our ordinary discourse when we interpret a person's behavior in causal terms with the awareness that we might be wrong or that other interpretations are possible. The difference between science and interpretation [hermeneutics] is that the dominant paradigm in science does not tolerate the presence of competing paradigms, whereas the realm of hermeneutics accommodates a heterogeneity of interpretation, which may be complementary or in conflict. The effect then of putting Freud on the terrain of interpretation or hermeneutics should be to minimize its coerciveness in both clinical practice and theoretical debates. The idolaters of Freud who proclaim the scientific validity of Freud's theory often confuse the question of interpretive difference with that of scientific validity. Thus the Freudian Paul Robinson rejects Jeffrey Masson's critique of Freud on the grounds that Masson holds a postmodern conception of the self in its infantile state as "both innocent and inert," whereas Freud's modernist view conceives of the self as "dangerously active."[15] (Robinson is suspicious of the ethos of victimhood that Masson's conception seems to endorse.) The point I wish to stress is that the difference between Robinson and Masson is one of interpretation: it cannot be adjudicated on scientific grounds.

Robinson's book *Freud and His Critics* is an interesting example of the misunderstandings that plague the controversies about Freud. In defending Freud against those whom he believes are his most formidable contemporary critics (Frank Sulloway, Jeffrey Masson and Adolf Grünbaum), Robinson defends his interpretation of Freud against the interpretation of his adversaries. According to Robinson, Frank Sulloway is wrong in reading Freud as a biologist of the mind because Freud's theory is irreducibly psychological, and Grünbaum is wrong in believing that Freud held that the validity of his theory depended on the success with which psychoanalysis effected cures. In these instances, Robinson has not demonstrated the scientific validity of Freud's thought; he has rather corrected or purported to correct misunderstandings of it. The vulnerability of Robinson's book lies not in the specific quarrels he has with Freud's critics, but in the illicit suggestion that he has in the process vindicated Freud's scientific credentials. In suggesting that science is not a fruitful site for considering the value of Freud's achievement, I don't mean to deny it the claim of knowledge or even truth. Only a scientistic view that holds that truth is the exclusive property of science would disbar us from considering the ways in which Freud's theory and the theories of others give us the truth of our psychological experience.

There is in psychoanalytic theory a qualification or check to the psychoanalyst's claim to authority: the confirming response of the analysand. The debate about where authority lies in psychoanalytic practice has been generated by what seems to me a false polarity. Habermas says the analysand, Grünbaum the analyst. These opposing views are half-right and half-wrong. The analysand lacks authority in the sense that he may not know his own motives; for an interpretation to work it needs the confirmation, both intellectual and emotional, of the analysand. Authority ideally is a transaction between analyst and patient. The analyst anticipates the patient in knowledge, the patient must give assent to what the analyst knows. We have already noted how Freud's argument for the primary importance of the incestuous content of *Oedipus Rex* is its capacity to stir a response in the audience, whereas other dramatic works that figure the conflict between human will and fate—the ostensible theme of *Oedipus Rex*—do not possess that capacity. One may ask again: How does Freud know that spectators are moved by the incestuous material and not by Oedipus' sense of victimization? If we transfer the method of proof to the psychoanalytic situation, another question arises: How can we be sure that an assent to an interpretation after the predictable initial "No" is the result of genuine self-discovery rather than the charismatic presence and insistence of the analyst?

Despite its potentiality for authoritarianism and coerciveness, the Freudian project maintains a respect for the person in his or her individuality as the Marxian project does not. For Marx the truth of a person lies not in his individuality but in his class character, of which he may not be conscious. As Harold Rosenberg points out, "class [for Marx] has character and individual physiognomy: the individual, independently of class has neither. The material relations in which individuals have existed until now have never permitted the human being to be himself. . . . The class is identical with that in the life of the individual which prevents him from being an individual. . . . The class is inescapably present to the individual as another self—it is the reality of his unreality."[16] Although Marx clearly views class as a self-alienating phenomenon, and clearly believes in a transcendence through which the individual will achieve substantial being and genuine freedom, the effect of the Marxian conception of individuals in a class society (the society we know) is imperiously to deny their existence and to disallow their voices, except in their relation to class.

Proceeding from other premises, Freud regards each individual as unique (not the same as unitary or coherent). The truth of his or her individuality whether in conscious or unconscious life is an individual truth. Freud, as we know, rejected the Jungian idea of a collective unconscious. The evidence for psychoanalytic discovery is to be found not in statistical averages (the typical person or the "abstract individual"), but in case histories of particular persons and their individual behavior, dreams, thoughts, and feelings. The difference is momentous for understanding and self-understanding.

In the Marxist view, the self comes to serve its class interest, which is conflated with its personal interest; in the Freudian view, the person must learn to extricate his personal interests from whatever alienates them in familial and social existence. The Freudian view that the person, not the collectivity of class, has primacy makes it ultimately inimical to a Marxist regime, a dangerous example of bourgeois thought and practice. Thus the clinical situation gives complete freedom to the analysand to express himself. "The true technique of psychoanalysis requires the physician to suppress his curiosity and leaves the patient complete freedom in choosing the order in which topics succeed each other during the treatment."[17] He may be directed to an understanding of himself that he did not intend, but he never becomes a mere figure in an ideological drama.

Patients are given freedom, but they are "free" to choose only what their unconscious dictates. If neurosis is the human condition, as Freud sometimes asserts, persons come to be seen as victims of psychic forces over which they have no control. The possibility of redemption lies in a collaboration between the acumen of the psychoanalytic interpreter and the willing susceptibility of the patient. The case histories provide us with portraits of human beings whose thoughts, feelings, and behavior are reducible to neuroses. Dora, we are told, is lively and intelligent, but what we see of her is nothing more than the manifestations of a neurotic condition. Freud would seem to be something of caricaturist of the psychic life. Here caricature need not have a pejorative meaning: it can refer to the exaggerations of certain features of psychological behavior so that they can be studied and understood and the patient cured of his neuroses.

It would, however, be a mistake to reduce Freud's achievement as a creator of character to the case histories. There is another category of human being that Freud evokes, the hero of mankind who has not submitted his psychic powers to some superior(?) being. His sublimations are not self-defeating symptoms but productive transformations of the libidinal energies of unconscious life. (Kenneth Burke has understood well Freud's appreciation of the sublimating needs of human beings.) Michelangelo's Moses, as Freud construes him, is a splendid instance of the transformation of libidinal energy.

> [Michelangelo] has modified the theme of the broken Tables; he does not let Moses break them in his wrath, but makes him be influ-

enced by the danger that they will be broken and calm that wrath, or
at any rate prevent it from becoming an act. In this way he has added
something new and more than human to the figure of Moses, so that
the giant frame with its tremendous physical power becomes only a
concrete expression of the highest mental achievement that is possible in a man, that of struggling successfully against an inward passion
for the sake of a cause to which he has devoted himself.[18]

Sublimation is the generative force of Freud's own symbolic imagination, as in his envisaging of the human world as a struggle
between Thanatos and Eros. The figures and tropes of Freudian
theoretical analysis constitute—they do not demystify—the world.
Freud, the narrative artist, elaborates reality rather than simplifying
it through reduction. The truth of persons is double for Freud:
their inchoate libidinal energy and their constitutive sublimating
capacity that Freud himself had in abundance. Freud's characterization of Moses is closer to a self-portrait than it is to what
Michelangelo intended. He may have thought of himself as having
replaced Moses as the lawgiver for the spiritual life of the modern
world.

Freud's assault on religion from the point of view of psychology
reenacts Marx's socioeconomic demystification of religion as "the
opiate of the people." (It also has affinities with the ideology critic
who treats literature as if it were an expression of cultural pathology.) It is the least impressive and appealing side of Freud's achievement, representing the worst of his Enlightenment legacy. Freud
was also suspicious of the sublimating tendencies of art and literature, but he did not repudiate them, because he discovered truths
in the works of artists that anticipated and confirmed his own findings and speculations. Why then should Freud have rejected the
insights of religious experience? His essay on Michelangelo's Moses
should have given him pause. In that essay and in *Civilization and
Its Discontents*, Freud's prose has a spiritual (might one say, a religious) elevation that belies his antireligious attitude. Unlike
William James, Freud seems to have only a negative knowledge of

the religious aspect of human psychology. In focusing on the object of belief as an illusion and failing to see the will to believe as the reality of millions of people, Freud the healer perversely deprived his audience, in particular his patients, of a source of consolation. Freud's horizon was defined by the limitations of his central European middle-class Enlightenment culture. That tradition had already divested itself of religious belief. Freud provided its agnosticism and atheism with a psychological theory.

I have not tried to absolve Freud of the charge of reductionism: there is a powerful reductionist tendency in his work, but this is not the whole story. There is also another tendency in which the will shows itself to be an indestructible faculty that guarantees the self and works invisibly to reconstruct it, sometimes in collaboration with a psychoanalyst and at other times heroically by itself. I have tried to explain the revisionist attack on Freud as an iconoclastic reaction against his iconic status in modern culture and suggest a view of his work that avoids idolatry and iconoclasm. What I have not done is explain why and how Freud achieved his unique authority in modern culture. Why Freud and not Weber, Durkheim or Tocqueville? Here's a speculation: Freud identified himself with Oedipus, who solved the riddle of the sphinx. In exploring the unconscious and its relation to conscious life, he thought he was defining the nature of man, and, to the extent that he succeeded—which is to say, to the extent that we recognize ourselves in the account that he provides, Freud must be the commanding figure of our culture in a way that Weber and Durkheim are not. Their achievements, great as they are, don't have a comparable ambition. So my earlier suggestion that he be demoted to a body of knowledge that includes Weber and Durkheim need not imply that one can distinguish his cultural status from theirs. It does mean, however, that like Weber or Durkheim or any figure in the history of culture, he should not be the ultimate arbiter of his own work.

How then should we judge his work? The answer depends on who the "we" are. Within psychoanalysis itself, Freud can be evaluated in the light of his own surpassing achievements. (I doubt whether any psychoanalytic theorist or practitioner exemplifies in a strict sense Foucault's view of Freudian discourse in which "a proposition's theoretical validity [is determined] by its relation to the work of the founder of the discourse.") From a scientific point of view, we should expect what Grünbaum and others expect: empirical verification, where appropriate and possible. We might also take a moral point of view and concern ourselves with Freud as a respecter of persons. Although Freud regards the person as unique, his doctrine of resistance in its imperial version betrays a disrespect for the self-understanding of the person. As with every great writer, however, we should be prepared to learn from and not only about him. We diminish him and ourselves if we simply test his work as it were from the outside, unwilling to follow him in his intellectual and imaginative flights. We need to follow Coleridge's and Mill's practice of asking what a text means before raising the question of whether it is true—and not underrate the difficulty of determining truth in psychological experience.

There may be something of an irony in my effort to save Freud the demystifier from demystification, that is, to separate the interpretive aspect of his work, which enhances understanding from its *coercive* reductiveness. I stress coercive because demystification and reduction have a role to play in our understanding, when it is not coercive.

CHAPTER EIGHT

The Passion of Reason: Reflections on Primo Levi and Jean Amery

You religious and enlightened people, you Christians, Jews, and Humanists, you believers in freedom, dignity and enlightenment— you think you know what a human being is. We will show you what he is, and what you are. Look at our camps and crematoria, and see if you can bring your hearts to care about these millions.[1]

The Holocaust has been the most formidable demystifier of our humanity. How impotent "freedom, dignity and enlightenment" seem in the face of its horrors. Does this mean that intellectual honesty demands that we surrender what appear to be the pretensions of humanity to these values? Or is it the case that a willingness to surrender these values would be an act of complicity with these horrors? These are not rhetorical questions. They are the most difficult of questions to answer. I have chosen to end my book with the experience of the Holocaust as reflected in the work of two of its wisest and most compelling survivors, because it puts to the test as no ideologically driven critique does those values of the Enlightenment that I have been trying to affirm.

The dominant wisdom about the Holocaust is that its enormity surpasses comprehension. Having shattered traditional faith (how could God have permitted it to happen?), the Holocaust has acquired the sanctity of deity and become the object of a kind of reverence. Like a religious mystery, the Holocaust has been shrouded with taboos. Silence is better than speech, because speech trivializes the mystery by representing the events in familiar terms. The sense of outrage that greeted Hannah Arendt's thesis about the banality of evil can be explained in part by the feeling that she had violated the mystery in translating the experience into the quotidian. Theodore Adorno writes from a sense of the sanctity of the experience, its unspeakableness, when he declares the impossibility and immorality of any writing about the Holocaust. The uniqueness of the Holocaust precludes comparisons, and comparison is essential to discourse. So better silence than speech or, if speech is inescapable, it must always know its limitations and finally confess its impotence. Speech is necessary, because total silence would mean oblivion and the moral imperative is never to forget.

I have no wish to minimize the enormity of the Holocaust nor to trivialize it with false comparisons. There is no greater intellectual and moral horror than contemporary efforts at Holocaust revisionism, which says either that the enormity has been exaggerated or that it never took place. But I cannot escape the impression that those who insist on the Holocaust as the modern version of the divine mystery (George Steiner among others), sui generis and intransitive, may be inadvertently mystifying what can be understood and explained. To speak or not to speak (in the manner of silence) in this way is paradoxically to threaten the Holocaust with a portentous verbal inflation that may deprive us of a moral discourse in which discriminations and judgments can be made. The fact is that the sacredness of the event is often displaced to the words that try to represent it. Writing or speech, not silence, becomes the medium of piety. For Steiner, the ideal reading of books and documents of survivors becomes an uncritical reverential act.

> These books and the documents that have survived are not for "review." Not unless "review" signifies, as perhaps it should in these instances, a "seeing-again," over and over. As in some Borges fable, the only completely decent "review" of the *Warsaw Diary* or of Eli Wiesel's *Night* would be to re-copy the book, line by line, pausing at the names of the dead and the names of the children as the orthodox scribe pauses, when re-copying the Bible, at the Hallowed name of God. Until we know many of the words by *heart* (knowledge deeper than usual) and can repeat a few at the break of morning to remind ourselves that we live *after*.[2]

But not all the witnesses mean to invite reverence. Survivors like Primo Levi and Jean Amery write from a strenuous moral point of view, springing from the rationalism of the classical Enlightenment. They have no quarrel with God, because they never believed in him. They do not claim to understand everything, for not everything is morally intelligible, but they do not deal in mysteries or wish to make them sacrosanct. They "respect" the mystery of the monstrous evil that produced the Holocaust, but that is not where their focus is. The moral intelligence can still engage the predicament and dilemmas of the victim. For them the question is: how is it possible to remain human in the grip of extremity? In the presence of mystery all one can do is to submit or to rage. Amery and Levi in their passionate commitment to moral reason (and their avoidance of matters of faith) speculate and invite us to speculate about the possibility of moral freedom. Above all, they wish to understand what can be understood, make comparisons where they are appropriate and the discriminations that are the basis for moral judgment. Their writings are characterized by an intellectual modesty that distinguishes them from the hubristic rationalism of the classical Enlightenment. They are as severe with the pretensions of a moral reason that believes it can master the world as any antirationalist critic, without, however, abandoning the cause of moral reason.

No one knows better than Levi or Amery how the cultured man, who has only the resources of a secular culture, often exhibits timidity, fear, even collaboration with the enemy in situations of totalitarian extremity. In the camps, Levi writes, "culture could be useful even if only in some marginal cases, and for brief periods; it could enhance an hour, establish a fleeting bond with a companion, keep the mind healthy. *It definitely was not useful in orienting oneself and understanding* [emphasis added]."[3] The lines of Levi that I have quoted come from an essay "The Intellectual at Auschwitz" in his posthumous collection of essays, *The Drowned and the Saved.* The occasion for the essay is a remarkable work of fellow survivor Jean Amery, *At the Mind's Limits,* in which Amery exposes the utter defenselessness of the agnostic intellectual. Without a trade or a craft, the intellectual was particularly vulnerable in his external situation. "In the camp he becomes an unskilled laborer, who had to do his job in the open—which meant in most cases that the sentence was already passed on him. . . . Camp life demanded above all bodily agility and physical courage that bordered on brutality,"[4] and the intellectual generally proved to be inadequate to the demand. But the internal situation was even worse. The intellectual found himself betrayed by the very qualities that were virtues outside of the camp: rationality, the questioning and self-questioning spirit. "Absolute intellectual tolerance and the methodological doubting of the intellectual became factors in his auto-destruction." Rational questioning turns upon itself, and the man of reason loses confidence in reason. Since skepticism of the radical kind teaches that there are no grounded natural rights or moral categories, power becomes its own justification.

The intellectual . . . who after the collapse of his initial inner resistance had recognized that what may not be, very well could be, who
experienced the logic of the SS as a reality that proved itself by the
hour, now took a few fateful steps further in his thinking. Were not
those who were preparing to destroy him in the right, owing to the
undeniable fact that they were the stronger ones?[5]

This is a devastating indictment, more severe than Levi's exposure
of the ineffectuality of the cultured man, but very much in the same
spirit. (The indictment resembles, though is not identical to, the
view held by Zygmunt Bauman, for instance, that a value-free rationality is the villain: that it explains the behavior of both the perpe-
trators and the victims who collaborated in their own demise.) The
criticism is all the more telling in the contrast both Levi and Amery
make between the fate of the agnostic and that of the believer. "The
non-agnostic, the believers in any belief whatsoever resisted the
seduction of power, provided, of course, they were not believers in
the National Socialist doctrine."[6] Unlike the intellectual who on
Amery's account becomes complicit in his own dehumanization
when he acknowledges the "rightness" of the power of his torturers,
the believer (whether Christian, Jewish or Marxist) remains morally
intact because he experiences himself as "part of a spiritual community that is interrupted nowhere, not even in Auschwitz."

In Amery in particular the sense of the pathos of the agnostic
intellectual verges on contempt, one is tempted to say self-contempt. But neither Amery nor Levi feels in the least tempted by the
faiths that sustain others. For them any faith seems to be a delusion
in the face of the evil they experienced in the concentration camp.
In Levi's words, "Actually, the experience of the Lager with its
frightful iniquity confirmed me in my non belief. It prevented, and
still prevents, me from conceiving of any form of providence or
transcendent justice."[7] And Amery for all his grudging admiration
for the believer who meets his fate with confidence has no curiosity
about "a religious grace that for me did not exist, or about an ide-

ology whose errors and false conclusions I felt I had seen through."[8] Amery's intellectual honesty and lucidity would make it morally impossible for him to embrace an ideology or a faith.

There may be something misleading in the severity with which Amery exposes the fecklessness and susceptibility to the temptations of power of the agnostic intellectual. Amery himself hardly exemplifies the intellectual who has capitulated to power. On the contrary, he displays throughout exemplary qualities of physical and moral courage. He describes an episode in which he traded blows with a torturer with the full knowledge that he would only suffer more blows, because it was the only way that he could preserve his own dignity:

> In Auschwitz he once hit me in the face because of a trifle; that is how he was used to dealing with all the Jews under his command. At this moment—I felt it with piercing clarity—it was up to me to go a step further in my prolonged appeals case against society. In open revolt I struck Juszek in the face in turn. My human dignity lay in this punch to his jaw—and that it was in the end I, the physically much weaker man, who succumbed and was woefully thrashed, meant nothing to me. Painfully beaten, I was satisfied with myself. But not, as one might think, for reasons of courage and honor, but only because I had grasped well that there are situations in life in which our body is our entire self and our entire fate. I was my body and nothing else: in hunger, in the blow that I suffered, in the blow that I dealt. My body, debilitated and crusted with filth, was my calamity. My body, when it tensed to strike, was my physical and metaphysical dignity.[9]

Amery seems immune to the temptations of power; indeed, his work breathes contempt for it. When he strikes back, it is not to display strength or power. His blows will only betray his vulnerability to the superior strength of the other, and he knows it. He strikes back because his dignity as a living being is at stake, and his dignity would not allow himself to be drawn down the path of a radical skepticism that would put his moral convictions in doubt.

This is a far cry from the logic of Amery's generic intellectual who acquiesces in his own destruction because might makes right. The danger, as Levi points out, is not that Amery, the agnostic intellectual will lose his soul to power, but that in his "courageous decision to leave the Ivory tower and go down into the battlefield," he will be led "to positions of such severity and intransigence as to make him incapable of finding joy in life, indeed of living."[10] Amery survived the camps only to take his own life.

How do we account for the contradiction between the portrait of the intellectual that Amery presents and Amery's own apparently disconfirming behavior? There is an implicit answer to the question in an essay he wrote in which he declares his allegiance to the classical enlightenment.

> I profess loyalty to enlightenment, specifically to the *classical* enlightenment—as a *philosophia perennis* that contains all of its own correctives, so that it is an idle game dialectically to dissect it. I stand up for analytical reason and its language, which is logic. In spite of all that we have had to experience, I believe that even today, as in the days of the Encyclopedists, knowledge leads to recognition and recognition to morality. And I maintain that it was not the Enlightenment that failed, as we have been assured ever since the first wave of the romantic counterenlightenment, but rather those who were appointed its guardians.[11]

Amery doesn't think of rationalism as an ideology or a faith, but in fact it functions as one: to speak of a *philosophia perennis* is to declare a belief in a world that can be challenged by moral reason, if not constituted by it. Amery would insist that his belief in reason is free of the mystifications of religious faith and Marxist ideology. It is a sign of mystification when a doctrine or dogma fails to perceive its own limitations, when it simply substitutes itself for the world.

Amery's rationalism knows its limitations as the doctrines of religion and Marxism do not. Yet he possesses what seems like an ideological conviction about reason that contrasts sharply with his portrait of the self-doubting intellectual. The insufficiency of rationalism consists in its opposition to instinct and passion. It is not reason, but, as Zygmunt Bauman points out, a kind of instinct that impelled the "rescuers [of concentration camp victims to act] in ways that were natural to them— spontaneously they were able to strike out against the horrors of their times."[12] Hannah Arendt and others have noted that one of the tasks of the Nazis in their preoccupation with the Holocaust was to root out "the animal pity by which all normal men are affected, in the presence of human suffering."[13] The critics of rationalism are right then to point to moral resistance that does not have its source in calculation or social construction. Rationalistic sociological explanation tends to repress the role of instinct and passion in the moral life. Nevertheless, reason retains its moral force in its ideal commitment to truth. Nazi ideology after all was based on consciously produced myths about Aryan superiority and lies about Jewish perfidy and inferiority. If the ideal of truth may not necessarily generate a will toward moral action, it is hard to conceive what such action would be without it. The insufficiency of reason as a motive for action does not argue against its human indispensability.

In any case, neither Amery nor Levi illustrates in himself the particular vulnerability of the agnostic intellectual to the ravages of the camps. Neither their integrity nor their survival is a function of their philosophy. Courage and cowardice and all the virtues and vices are matters of character. Philosophies may authorize virtues, but they do not determine character. But a philosophy *is* an instrument of understanding, and the effect of Amery's and Levi's rationalism is to keep alive a kind of moral discourse in response to extremity that the Holocaust was supposed to have made impossible. Without ever losing respect for the enormity of the event, without minimizing the suffering, their own suffering, they are singularly free of a kind of piety before the event that paralyzes understanding or leads to self-righteousness. Both Amery and Levi apply to their experiences the "corrective" of the moral intelligence. Their aim is to describe what occurred with the greatest accuracy and truthfulness. This is the task of the witness. But that is not all. As survivors of the event, they feel compelled to represent and understand their responses both at the time of their incarceration and after their liberation. The witness is not a generic character, indistinguishable from other witnesses. He is a particular individual, with a particular cast of mind and capacity for feeling. What appears in *At the Mind's Limits* and *The Drowned and the Saved* are the extraordinary characters of men who emerged from the crucible of the Holocaust. ("Crucible" is an ironic concession to the murderers, for they thought of their monstrous project as an experiment.) Part of *our* witness as readers is to contemplate the characters of Levi and Amery and to meditate critically on their understanding and self-understanding.

In bringing together Levi and Amery, I don't mean to conflate their views. It would violate the truth to homogenize the survivors of the Holocaust, even if they happen to be of the same philosophical persuasion. To do so would deny them the differences that mark them as individuals. Amery is driven by the emotion of resentment, Levi is not. In fact, it is Amery's resentment that troubles Levi's response to him. As a moral philosopher, Amery knows well the risks of resentment and he defends the emotion with full knowledge of the criticism. Resentment, Nietzsche and Max Scheler have taught us, is the emotion of the weak and the victimized. The resentment accumulates, becoming, in Scheler's words, "an evil secretion in a sealed vessel, like prolonged impotence."[14] The desire for justice turns into a desire for revenge and the sense of justice disappears. Resentment is the emotion that nourishes revolutionary ideologies and only too often, as history shows, the revolutionary sense of justice. Amery of course knows the literature of and about resentment, but in what may appear to his readers an exercise in perversity, he affirms his own inextinguishable resentment and insists on its moral value. The targets of Amery's resentmcnt are not only the criminals who committed monstrous and unpardonable crimes against humanity but also a whole nation, which in its indifference or timidity or sheer cowardice or robotic obedience allowed these crimes to occur. Amery embraces the discredited doctrine of "collective guilt." He recognizes the possible pathology of his feelings, but he does not wish to concede his case prematurely to the psychologists. What does he mean to accomplish with his resentment? Its main object is the German good conscience that seems to have accompanied the prosperity that has risen from the ashes of Germany's defeat.

> It was not at all necessary that in German towns Jewish cemeteries and monuments for resistance fighters be desecrated. Conversations like the one I had in 1958 with a Southern German businessman over breakfast in the hotel were enough. Not without first politely inquiring whether I was an Israelite, the man tried to convince me that there was no longer any race hatred in his country. The German people bear no grudge against the Jewish people, he said. As proof he cited his government's magnanimous policy of reparations, which was, incidentally, well appreciated by the young state of Israel.

Amery cannot abide what he perceives to be self-satisfaction and lack of remorse, though he feels miserable in contemplating himself as a "Shylock, demanding his pound of flesh."[15]

His resentment is ultimately a grievance against "the antimoral natural process of healing that time brings about, and by which I make the genuinely humane and absurd demand that time be turned back" (77). The torturers or *some* of them have been punished: we are reminded of those who have escaped punishment and prospered. And what of their descendants? "To accuse the young would be just too inhuman, and according to universal concepts also unhistorical" (75), writes this scrupulous resentful man. But he wants them to mistrust themselves if not to suffer the guilt of their parents: the moral equation Amery envisages is resentment in the victim and self-mistrust in the "opposite camp." The most devastating effect of sadistic torture on Amery's psyche is the loss of "trust in the world." Amery would "avenge" himself on the country that bred these torturers by inducing self-mistrust in the descendants of the torturers. He wants what he calls the "unresolved conflict between victims and slaughterers [to be] externalized and actualized," although he never makes clear what externalization or actualization would entail. Historical memory is required if history is not to repeat itself and historical memory means self-mistrust. Amery does not consider the possible price of a deep and persistent self-mistrust in the opposite camp, which can turn into a destructive counterresentment. By wanting to reverse history in order to produce the German revolution that never took place, he is asking for the impossible, and he knows it when he speaks of his "genuinely humane and *absurd* demand" [emphasis added] (77). Of course, Amery's resentments need to be distinguished from the Nietzschean conception, which owes a great deal to Dostoevsky's underground man. Resentment, according to Nietzsche, luxuriates in imaginary grievances. There is nothing imaginary in Amery's resentments. Resentment declares itself against injustice, but is itself the source of injustice in its false accusations or in the disparity between the provocation and the emotion. No emotion is adequate to the enormity of the event that is the object of Amery's emotion. What Amery has in common with the resentful man is the futility of his passion.

Toward the end of the essay on "Resentments," Amery writes: "Perhaps already tomorrow it will lead me to self-condemnation, by having me see the moral desire for reversal as the half-brained chatter that it already is today for the rationally thinking know-it-alls" (81). Amery, the rationalist, concedes the possible irrationality of his view, but there is implicit criticism of a comfortable rationalism that provides no vent for moral indignation. In its protest against nature ("the natural process of healing"), Amery's resentment dramatizes the monstrous character of the Holocaust. The wound inflicted will not heal with time; it is too deep, too awful, too terrible for the patience of time. The resentment itself is a wound, one of the deepest that the rational man can suffer. Amery's resentment illuminates the Holocaust as a premature rational response does not. The visceral nonideological character of Amery's resentments has compelling power, in great part because of the unparalleled enormity of the Holocaust and the system that bred it. Moreover, unlike the ideology critics who often desire the power and authority they decry in their adversaries, Amery in his resentments is singularly devoid of the desire for power. The risks incurred by his resentments are mainly internal. Since resentment is an emotion that one does not act on, it can fester and turn on the resenter, wearing away at the fiber of his being and perhaps destroy him. Resentment is an emotion compatible with suicide, as Levi himself remarks when he comments on "the positions of . . . severity and intransigence [that Amery took, which made] him incapable of finding joy in life, indeed of living."

In persisting in his resentments, does Amery in effect capitulate to the horror of the camps? He never conceded rightness to power as did the agnostic intellectuals he describes, but in taking his own life he may have implied that there is no self-sustaining answer to that power. Torture, he asserts, undermines one's "trust in the world"; it devalues the world for the victim, so even if the victim survives, the torturer has accomplished his goal. Amery describes sadism (the "philosophy" of the torturer) as the desire "to nullify this world" and "realize his own total sovereignty" (35). By conceding the overwhelming power of the torturer over mind as well as body, Amery has apparently conceded victory to the torturer. For the survivor or a certain kind of survivor the triumph over Nazism changed nothing. The sadist posthumously accomplishes his task of annihilating the world.

But one may understand the logic of suicide differently. In acknowledging the overwhelming power of the Holocaust, it declares its radical refusal to abide it, to live within it. Suicide becomes an act of integrity, an implicit affirmation of the values the camps have rendered impossible. (One should not confuse survival with integrity. Levi remarks that the worst often survived, the worst being the cleverest, the most opportunistic, and the luckiest. We know that Levi, like many other survivors, never overcame his guilt for having survived.)

Terrence Des Pres has made a case for survival itself as a value for life in extremity. Against the view expressed by Bruno Bettelheim and others that ideals justify life and that one should be prepared to die for a cause, Des Pres affirms the survivor's "code" that life justifies ideals. But what does life itself signify? Des Pres offers examples of Dostoevsky and Bertrand Russell, who, close to death, experience a recovery (in Dostoevsky's case, a last-minute reprieve from a death sentence) and testify to the delight and value of simply being alive. But Des Pres's examples seem irrelevant to the situation of life in the camps, where the threat (the word is too weak) is not simply to one's existence.[16] The aim of the camps is "to reduce us to beasts" (Levi); dehumanization, not death, is the worst that can befall a human being, which is the reason it is important to have an ideal of what it means to be human. And one's humanity entails a capacity to "refuse consent," to resist the effort of the torturers to turn one into a beast. The willingness to die, even to take one's life, may be preferable to survival.

The logic of suicide can be resisted, as Levi resisted it *in his writing*, by an understanding of the world as not wholly defined by the extremity in which both Levi and Amery found themselves in the years of the Holocaust. The permanent value of Amery is that he dramatizes a real possibility, not an inevitability, that the world can be transformed into an extremity in which life itself becomes worthless. The testimony to that worthlessness reflects a realm of value which extremity has temporarily expunged.

The testimony survives and it tells us that the moral vulnerability of the agnostic intellectual, the person of culture, is not absolute. Both Levi and Amery exhibit in their writing a combination of character, intelligence, learning, and eloquence that apparently survived the degradation of the camps. Even Amery, even Amery cannot disburden himself of the culture that proved so useless to him in the camps. His meditations are saturated with philosophical and literary culture. Goethe, Hegel, Sartre, Mann: they belong to the spiritual authority that makes us attend so closely to his writing. There are telling references to literature in Levi's effort to understand what occurred in the camps as in his quotation of a passage from *Measure for Measure*, which provides him with an image of despotic authority:

> Dressed in a little brief authority
> Most ignorant of what he's most assured,
> His glassy essence, like an angry ape
> Plays such fantastic tricks before high heaven
> As makes the angels weep.[17]

This is after the fact, less compelling than the way cultural memory, Dante, for example, performed in Levi's mind, while he was in the camps. Memories of Dante were of "great value. They made it possible for me to reestablish a link with the past, saving it from oblivion and reinforcing my identity. They convinced me that my mind, although besieged by everyday necessities, had not ceased to function. They elevated me in my own eyes and those of my interlocutor. They granted me a respite, ephemeral but hebetudinous, in fact liberating and differentiating; in short, a way to find myself."[18]

He devotes a chapter to the "Canto of Ulysses" in *Survival at Auschwitz*, recalling that a particular passage suddenly and inexplicably came to mind:

> Then of that age-old fire loftier born
> Began to mutter and move, as a wavering
>   flame
> Wrestles against the wind and is over-born;
> And, like a speaking tongue vibrant to
>   flame
> Language, the tip of it flickering to and
>   fro
> Threw out a voice and answered: "When
>   I came...."

He expresses puzzlement about "how or why it came into my mind."[19] The passage becomes a sort of mantra (if we can speak of the complexity and elaborateness of Levi's recollection of the passage as a mantra), enabling him to defy the circumstances of his existence and sustain him. One does not have to know how the passage came to Levi's mind to be struck by how apt the memory of *The Inferno* is in the circumstances. Levi does not evoke the images of horror and degradation in the poem, beings frozen in ice, buried in excrement, suffering the most excruciating pain and without the promise of an end. *The Inferno* could be the poem of the Holocaust, were it not for the fact that even in hell the image of the human is preserved. It was Erich Auerbach, a refugee from Naziism, who revealed the extraordinary humanity of the condemned figures in hell. Severe as divine punishment may be, they retain their human capacity. Dante's characters are given the "freedom" to relive their earthly pasts in imagination, a permanently recurrent hell defying imagination. When the pilgrim Dante encounters them, their pasts, filled with suffering of a kind different from what they experience in hell, provoke his sympathy and we remember them as they lived in the world. *The Inferno* in its intensity helps us see the even more radical extremity of the Holocaust. Dante's hell is, after all, the work of an imagination, that of Dante's God, which also conceived purgatory and paradise. Purgatory and paradise are inconceivable in the mind that produced the Holocaust. Levi in effect becomes a character in a hell worse than Dante's and, unlike Dante's character, undeserving of a place in it. Like Dante's characters, Levi "proves" in his very being the inextinguishability of the human face.

What separates Amery and Levi is the character of their judgments. Amery's sense of extremity *tends* to divide the world sharply between victim and tormentor; he is less interested in the range of intermediate behavior that occurs in what Levi calls the gray zone. How, one might ask, can one question a sense of extremity where the Holocaust is concerned? Doesn't justice demand the utmost rigor in condemning the trimmers as well as the torturers, the compromisers as well as those who inflicted cruelties? It is difficult to regard these questions as anything but rhetorical. And yet they go to the heart of the difference between Amery and Levi. Levi's essay on "The Gray Zone" exhibits "pity and rigor" and a sensitivity to "extenuating circumstances" in the cases of people who compromised or did not resist, which has no parallel in the work of Amery.

Levi focuses on the victims of the system who were degraded into collaboration: for instance, the *sonderkommandos*, the special squad of "privileged" inmates who were given enough to eat for a few months as a reward for the task of running the crematoria. He acknowledges the horror, but he is not quick to judge or rather is quick only to judge the terrible system that turns even the victims to the performance of monstrous tasks:

> Every human being possesses a reserve of strength whose extent is unknown to him, be it large, small, or nonexistent, and only through extreme adversity can we evaluate it. Even apart from the extreme case of the Special Squads, often those of us who have returned, when we describe our vicissitudes, hear in response: "In your place I would not have lasted for a single day." This statement does not have a precise meaning: one is never in another's place. Each individual is so complex that there is no point in trying to foresee his behavior, all the more so in extreme situations; nor is it possible to foresee one's own behavior. Therefore I ask that we meditate on the story of "the crematorium ravens" with pity and rigor, but that judgment of them be suspended.[20]

Levi's suspension of judgment is not an exercise in self-indulgence. It represents the moral sanity that the camps tried to and did extinguish. It is an answer to what Levi imagines to be the psychological self-justifying strategy (the rationale) of the Final Solution. "We, the master race, are your destroyers, but you are no better than we are; if we so wish, and we do so wish, we can destroy not only your bodies but also your souls, just as we have destroyed ours."[21]

The gray zone is a feature of the moral life everywhere, but it has particular poignancy in situations of extremity. In ordinary situations, people who conduct their lives in the gray zone are often the object of contempt for their equivocations and compromises, or their failure to choose or decide find little justification in the world outside themselves. We often speak of these justifications as rationalizations. The equivocations and failures reflect moral ineffectuality or cowardice. But the gray zone in the camps exists in a realm beyond risk or the efficacy of character. The effort of the camps is to reduce human beings to the level of sheer need in which choice or agency of any kind becomes virtually impossible. The camps are the ultimate machines of determinism. This may be to state the case hyperbolically, because even in the most extreme totalitarian situations there is some porousness, some room for maneuver. But the fact remains that the camps effectively eliminate the conditions of moral life.

So we are in the presence of something of a paradox when the moral intelligence retrospectively engages the events. Surely people reacted differently from one another to the events and their reactions proceeded from differences of character, some people behaving more admirably than others. But the radical reduction in the possibility of action, the extremity of suffering, the lack of time for reflection, existence being a continuous state of emergency: all these circumstances must produce in those who view the events from the comfort of ordinary life pity rather than judgment. When Levi speaks of rigor he means, I believe, a rigor that works as an antidote against facile condemnations of "sins" or "crimes" of the victims. Such rigor should serve the most important distinction of all: that between the tormentor and the victim. The peril to be avoided at all cost is to allow an understanding of the powerful determinism that defined the camps to excuse the behavior of those who ran them, for they exist irredeemably beyond the gray zone. According to Tzvetan Todorov, in his heroic effort to understand and not simply judge, Levi did not entirely avoid the peril. Understanding the tormentor, Todorov argues with compassion for Levi, may not be the task for the survivor.[22]

I don't mean to diminish the penetration and complexity of

Amery's moral intelligence. But his imagination is powerfully shaped and determined by the experience of extremity as Levi's is not. I must be careful to qualify this distinction. Levi's work is, of course, pervasively influenced by the Holocaust, but his temperament does not have the same susceptibility to extremity. If Amery is the man of reason, Levi is the reasonable man. He himself summed it up beautifully in speaking of Amery's suicide:

> It was not commented on, it was not "comforted by tears." In the face of death, in the habit of death, the frontier between culture and lack of culture disappeared. Amery states that one no longer thought about *whether* one would die, an accepted fact, but rather about *how*. "There were discussions about the time necessary for the poison in the gas chambers to take effect. There were speculations about the painfulness of death by phenol injection. Should one hope for a blow on the skull or death by exhaustion in the infirmary?" On this point my experience and my recollections diverge from Amery's. Perhaps because I was younger, perhaps because I was more ignorant than he, or less marked, or less conscious, I almost never had time to devote to death. I had many other things to keep me busy—finding a bit of bread, avoiding exhausting work, patching my shoes, stealing a broom, or interpreting the signs and faces around me. The aims of life are the best defense against death: and not only in the Lager.[23]

For this reason, Levi's own death (we are no longer sure it was suicide) remains shrouded in mystery.

My reading of *The Drowned and the Saved* is at odds with Cynthia Ozick's interpretation of the book as a "suicide note." She makes a metaphor of the trading of blows in characterizing the book as "one of the blows returned by a pen of fire." No longer the objective writer who cultivates "magisterial equanimity, unaroused detachment,"[24] Levi now releases his pent up rage against his tormentors and writes "the bitterest of suicide notes." This reading of Levi seems to me misconceived, especially coming from so acute a reader as Ozick. It is in *The Drowned and the Saved* that Levi rebukes, if that is the right word, Amery's self-destructive retaliatory impulses as the sign of someone preoccupied with death and remarks in contrast his own devotion to the aims of life. Levi had always managed to combine equanimity with a moral lucidity that knew when to judge and with what degree of severity and when to suspend judgment. *The Drowned and the Saved* exhibits these qualities throughout; if there are "lapses" as in his anger toward apparently well-meaning Germans who write to explain themselves to him, they seem hardly to justify the notion that Levi is announcing his suicide. But even if it is true that Levi shows an aggressiveness in the book not to be found in his previous work, the identification of that aggressiveness with the literal trading of blows in Amery confuses fact with metaphor. To trade blows in the camps is to invite death. To deliver blows in a book against a defeated but still dangerous enemy may be an affirmative, even life-affirming act. Ozick would not have arrived at her conclusions about *The Drowned and the Saved* before the fact of Levi's "suicide." There is a kind of irresponsible reading of a text that invents from a merely literary interpretation a history that requires evidence of another sort. (Leslie Fiedler's ascertaining of the guilt of the Rosenbergs from their letters to one another strikes me as another such example.) In Ozick's case, the irresponsibility is compounded by fact that we are not sure that Levi committed suicide (hence the quotation marks above) or, if he did, we do not know and should not presume to know what the reasons were, since there was no suicide note.

Suicide is the negation of survival. We may be missing the lesson of the Lager by allowing the ethic of survival to provide the focus for discussion. To suggest that the mere capacity for survival reflects *moral* integrity is to insult the countless admirable people who perished in the Holocaust. The lesson of the Lager concerns the question of what it tells us about the nature of people forced to live in the conditions created by the Lager. For Levi, the answer is *not* that man is "fundamentally brutal, egoistic and stupid in his conduct once every civilized institution is taken away, and that the Haftling is consequently nothing but a man without inhibitions." Such a vicw allows what Levi sardonically calls the experiment to define the human condition; it erodes the distinction between victimizer and victim by accepting the view that the victim in his dehumanization is no better than the master race. Levi draws a different conclusion: "that in the face of driving necessity and physical disabilities many social habits and instincts are reduced to silence."[25] Social habits and instincts constitute the essence of our humanity. The camps had as their aim the destruction of that essence, and it achieved its aim to the extent that it persuaded people that man is fundamentally, or by nature, brutal. The Nazis meant to show not merely that their victims were beasts in stripping them of their humanity: humanity itself becomes contemptible. Nazi genocide had as its ultimate logic the destruction of humanity. Serial killers, the Nazis tried systematically to destroy all the peoples of the earth, leaving only the Aryan, who is "more" than human. To be neither a human being nor a beast is not to be a superman, as the Aryan saw himself, but a monster.

It is for this reason that Levi is careful to note instances of people who managed to preserve their integrity and decency, no matter how extreme conditions were:

> I believe that it was really due to Lorenzo that I am alive today; and not so much for his material aid as for his having constantly reminded me by his presence, by his natural and plain manner of being good, that there still existed a just world outside our own, something and someone still pure and whole, not corrupt, not savage, extraneous to hatred and terror, something difficult to define, a remote possibility of good, but for which it was worth surviving.[26]

The testimony of Levi and others should caution us against the perniciousness of recent efforts to deconstruct and demystify "the human" in the putative interest of truth.

Yet it is true that moral reason or the cultural tradition is too weak a resource in extreme situations. It does not provide the sense of solidarity that one discovers among believers and ideologues. Contemporary critics of the Enlightenment have focused on the poverty of the communal imagination of Enlightenment thought, although in theory the Enlightenment promises fraternity. The site of enlightened reason is the individual person whose sense of community with others may be abstract. In contrast, a confirmed Communist, like Levi's barber "never despaired," because "Stalin was his fortress, the Rock sung in the psalms."[27] The communal imperative can, of course, become a tyranny. Utopian constructions, when realized, may turn out to be communities of terror. All "solutions" proposed by the moral intelligence to the abiding threat of extremity remain provisional and precarious, requiring an anxious vigilance. But the obvious "inadequacy" of the solutions may be the only alternative to the intolerable "demystification" of our humanity by the Holocaust.

CONCLUDING REMARKS

In a recent manifesto, "Speaking for the Humanities," a committee of distinguished literary scholars represented "contemporary humanist thinking [at its best as] not [peddling] ideology, but rather attempt[ing] to sensitize us to the presence of ideology and its capacity to delude us into promoting as universal values that in fact belong to one nation, one social class, one sect."[1] In an earlier draft circulated to directors of humanities centers, the word "omnipresence" appears instead of "presence." One can only speculate about the reason for the change. Another sentence in the published report may provide a clue. "One need not make an absolute commitment to the view that no thought can be 'uncontaminated' by interests in order to see how intellectually fruitful that view can be."[2] The authors seem to have recognized that "omnipresence" might be overreaching, but they nevertheless wish to capitalize on it. If it is not necessarily true that ideology is everywhere, it is "intellectually fruitful" to assume that it is. But why should it be fruitful to employ an assumption that one suspects might not be true? It is more reasonable to suppose that it will distort rather than illuminate.

The authors of the report do not explain how their own approach escapes the contamination of ideology. I have tried to show that this kind of systematic attempt at making us aware of ideological delusions is itself an exercise in ideology of the most aggressive kind, for it posits without argument a world in which universals do not, indeed cannot exist, in which reason becomes rationalization and in which god terms that speak of transcendence are mystifications.

The answer to ideology critique should not be a dogmatic and unargued affirmation of universals, reason and transcendence, in effect replicating the unearned conviction that the ideology critics possess the truth. One needs to be an ideology critic to realize how vulnerable a universalist discourse is. One need *not* be one to acknowledge how the loss of universals diminishes the world and to remain open to a version of universality that makes possible dialogue among perspectives. It is difficult to see how such communication is possible among ideology-driven nations, social classes and sects without an ideal of universality.

It would, however, be a mistake to infer from my argument a complete repudiation of ideological interpretation. Like any other approach to texts and institutions, it has productive uses. The mistrust of appearances, the demystifier's stock-in-trade, when it doesn't become systematic or paranoiac, is necessary to one's mental equipment. My ambivalent admiration of Freud acknowledges both the power and the distortions of his unmasking procedures. The quarrel I have with ideology critique (it is also Kenneth Burke's) concerns its imperial presumption that there is nothing but ideology. Such a view leaves no room for aesthetic or moral or cultural criticism. It simply preempts the whole field of cultural study.

Of the writers who seem closest to the spirit of Enlightenment universalism, only Jean Amery, the Holocaust survivor, and Alain Finkielkraut embrace it in its classic expression. The others I refer to—Kolakowski, Gellner, Berlin, and Todorov—perceive limitations and difficulties. Kolakowski consciously commits the inconsistency of formulating a limited universalism to protect Enlightenment values from barbarism. He further limits his commitment by subjecting the Enlightenment to a critique from a religious perspective, the perspective that the classic Enlightenment tried to demystify. (It is an irony of modern cultural history that the Enlightenment itself is the source of the kind of critique that seeks to undo it.) I have made much of Kolakowski, Berlin, and Todorov because in their self-critical openness and flexibility they represent an alternative way of thinking to what has become the fairly predictable exercise of ideological interpretation. The way we think is not merely a matter of academic interest. As Levi and Amery show, what may be at stake is the survival of the very idea of humanity.

In chastising the hubris of ideology critique (an activity of the cultural left), one need not repudiate all the social and cultural changes that have taken place in recent years. This is the attitude of neoconservatives, who rarely engage the arguments of the left, because they regard them as beneath contempt. In doing so, they commit the sin of exclusion in peremptorily declaring certain views beyond the pale, precisely what its adversaries do. There are contemptible arguments, but they should not be made to exhaust the range of thought possible to liberal or left perspectives. There are, I should note as well, contemptible arguments on the conservative side. The identification of the debasement of a position with the position itself does no service to the intellectual life.

The interest in cultural diversity, the emergence of the women's movement, the changing character of the student body—these are facts of our cultural life. A number of intellectuals respect these facts and have been thinking and writing creatively and unfashionably about the current situation, among them Kolakowski and Todorov. Their work is distinguished by a rare combination of respect for difference and a belief in the idea of a common humanity. Both writers have experienced imperialist oppression, although not from the West, the agent of imperialism usually invoked in the academy. Their skepticism, which protects them against dogmatism, is not of the radical kind that makes genuine conviction impossible. In their rethinking of the Enlightenment, they represent a belief in the values of reason, intellectual honesty and clarity as the foundations of our cultural life. They are signs of a possible future.

NOTES

Introduction

1. Hans Barth, *Truth and Ideology* (Berkeley: University of California Press, 1976), 162.

2. It is Friedrich Engels, who launched the career of "false consciousness" in *Letter to Mehring*, 1893. "Ideology is a process accomplished by the so-called thinker consciously indeed but with a false consciousness. The real motives impelling him remain unknown to him, otherwise it would not be an ideological process at all. Hence, he imagines false or apparent motives. Because it is a process of thought, he derives both its form and its content from pure thought, either his own or his predecessors'." See Raymond Williams, *Keywords* (New York: Oxford University Press, 1983), 155.

3. Gregory Jay, "Ideology and the New Historicism," *Arizona Quarterly* (Spring 1991): 143.

4. Terry Eagleton, "Criticism and Politics: The Work of Raymond Williams," *New Left Review* (January–February 1976): 23.

5. Louis Althusser, *For Marx* (London: Verso, 1990), 232.

6. Ibid., 69.

7. Robert Alter's *The Pleasures of Reading in an Ideological Age* (New York: Simon & Schuster, 1989) is an exemplary effort to save texts (their surfaces and depths) from those who would transform them into ideological structures.

8. See Stephen Carter, *Reflections of an Affirmative Action Baby* (New York: Basic Books, 1992), 29.

9. Edward Said, *Culture and Imperialism* (New York: Random House, 1994), 70–71.

10. Ibid., 189.

11. See Aijaz Ahmad, *In Theory: Classes, Nations, Literatures* (London: Verso, 1992), 168.

12. See, for example, Rob Nixon, *London Calling: V. S. Naipaul, Postcolonial Mandarin* (New York: Oxford University Press, 1992). The obsession with colonialism and imperialism in effect prevents Nixon from taking seriously Naipaul's criticism of the ethos of postcolonial societies. All failures in those societies are reflexively and exclusively attributed to the legacy of the departed imperial powers.

13. With great brio, D. A. Miller's *The Novel and the Police* (Berkeley: University of California Press, 1988) makes the most impressive case for the policing and disciplinary function of the novel as a genre and form. The book is filled with subtle local insights into the novels he studies and amounts to a significant contribution to our understanding of nineteenth-century fiction. But Miller's demystification of the view that the novel is an open form, expressed, for instance, in Roger Caillois's assertion that there is a "contradiction between the idea of the police and the nature of the novel" (quoted on p. 6) is itself an ideological construction. This can be seen more clearly in critics of lesser talent who ritualistically make his argument or rather repeat his view without arguing it, as if its truth has already been established for all those with eyes to see.

14. See Wayne Booth, *The Company We Keep: An Ethics of Fiction* (Berkeley: University of California Press, 1988), 443.

15. Chinua Achebe, *Morning Yet on Creation Day* (New York: Doubleday, 1975), 10.

16. Said, *Culture and Imperialism*, 126.

17. See Harold Bloom, *The Western Canon* (New York: Harcourt Brace, 1994).

1. From Culture to Ideology

1. Terry Eagleton, *Ideology: An Introduction* (London: Verso, 1991), 28.

2. T. S. Eliot, *Notes Toward a Definition of Culture* (New York: Harcourt Brace, 1949), 30.

3. I don't share Alain Finkielkraut's mistrust of culture as a category inimical to reason. In *The Defeat of the Mind* (New York: Columbia University Press, 1995), 96–97, he traces the anthropological extension of culture, which includes "all the customs and skills learned by man as a member of a group," to the romantic counter-Enlightenment inaugurated by Herder. The fate of culture in the English tradition has been quite different from that in the European. Matthew Arnold conceives of culture and reason as inextricably bound up in each other. For him culture embodies reason and the will of God. T. S. Eliot favors an anthropological conception of culture, but does not display a counter-Enlightenment hostility to reason. Eliot's philosophical training, the influence of his teacher Irving Babbitt, his classical temperament may have all played a part in keeping him apart from irrationalism, which is not to say that Eliot belongs in the rationalist tradition. The opposition between culture and reason, as formulated by Finkielkraut, may be a category mistake.

4. The cultural idea depends on the possibility of decontextualization and recontextualization. But so long as it remains merely a possibility, culture has all the liabilities of an abstraction. George Eliot provides an image of culture that betrays its vulnerability while celebrating it. "Felix Holt's face had the look of habitual meditative abstraction from objects of mere personal vanity or desire, which is the peculiar stamp of culture, and makes a roughly cut face worthy to be called the human face divine" (*Felix Holt, The Radical*, edited by Fred C. Thomson [Clarendon: Oxford University Press, 1980], 248.)

5. Eagleton, *Ideology*, 166.

6. John Thompson, *Studies in the Theory of Ideology* (Berkeley: University of California Press, 1984), 5.

7. Raymond Geuss has distinguished among three uses of ideology: descriptive, positive, and pejorative. It is the rare writer who in using the terms avoids blurring the distinctions among its several uses. What provokes ideology critique, however, is its pejorative sense of ideology in which distortion, falsification, and masking are allegedly at play. See *The Idea of a Critical Theory* (Cambridge: Cambridge University Press, 1981).

8. Eagleton, *Ideology*, 168.

9. Ibid., xi.

10. See Paul Ricoeur, *Lectures on Ideology and Utopia*, edited by George H. Taylor (New York: Columbia University Press, 1986), 157.

11. Raymond Williams gives a succinct account of the historical vicissitudes of "ideology" from the time of its invention by the French rationalist philosopher Destutt de Tracy to its Marxist uses. For de Tracy, ideology is the philosophy of mind. Napoleon initiates its modern negative meaning as false consciousness by attributing it to the exponents of popular democracy "who misled the people by elevating them to a sovereignty which they were incapable of exercising." In Marxism, ideology plays an ambiguous role as the false consciousness of the ruling class and as a relatively neutral term characterizing the thought and practice of a class, whether it be the bourgeois or the proletarian class. Raymond Williams, *Keywords*, 153–157. See also Emmet Kennedy, *A Philosophe in the Age of Revolution: Destutt de Tracy and the Origins of Ideology* (Philadelphia: The American Philosophical Society, 1978). In recent years, culture and ideology have become entwined in anthropological discussion in both the negative and the relatively neutral senses in ways that are often difficult to sort out.

12. Kenneth Burke, *Permanence and Change*, rev. ed. (Berkeley: University of California Press, 1984), 294.

13. Hans Barth, *Truth and Ideology* (Berkeley: University of California Press, 1976), 162.

14. The habit of inverting meanings, of showing how an underlying motive contradicts surface meaning and hence becomes the real meaning of the text, is a habit of reducing a higher or generous meaning to a lower or meaner motive, but occasionally it works the other way, when a friend or ally is involved. Thus Fredric Jameson, concerned to protect Paul de Man against the charge of anti-Semitism, transforms the plain sense of de Man's article into an act of resistance to anti-Semitism.

As for the notorious "anti-Semitic" article, I believe that it has been consistently misread: it strikes me as the ingenious effort at resistance of a young man altogether too smart for his own good. For the message of this "intervention" is the following: "you garden-variety anti-Semites and intellectuals (we will leave the lofty "religious" anti-Semitism of the Third Reich out of it) in fact do your own cause a disservice. You have not understood that if "Jewish literature" is as dangerous and virulent as you claim it is, it follows that Aryan literature does not amount to much, and in particular lacks the stamina to resist a Jewish culture which is supposed to be, under other canonical "anti-Semitic" accounts, valueless. You would therefore under these circumstances be better advised to stop talking about the Jews altogether and to cultivate your own garden.

Postmodernism or, The Cultural Logic of Late Capitalism (Durham: Duke University Press, 1991), 258.

The possibility of such a reading peremptorily becomes the truth of what de Man meant (there is no real evidence offered to support such a reading) and the basis for a dismissal of more plausible interpretations. It is characteristic of the kind of ideology critique I am describing that the critic doesn't simply offer his reading as a possible one among others but that it is intended to sweep the field.

15. Jameson, *Postmodernism,* 180. If everything is ideology, the meaning of the word becomes blurred or slippery and a cognate like *ideologue* loses its meaning. How can we speak of someone as an ideologue if everyone is in a sense defined by ideology? Is it sheer illusion that those of us who do not think of ourselves as ideologues have had the experience of knowing one when we meet one? In contrast to Jameson, Althusser limits the province of ideology. "Ideology *has no outside* (for itself), but at the same time . . . *it is nothing but outside* (for science and reality)" (*Ideology and Ideological State Apparatuses* [1970] translated by Ben Brewster in *Contemporary Critical Theory,* edited by Dan Latimer [New York: Harcourt Brace, 1989], 97). Those who inhabit an ideology live under the illusion that there is nothing outside it. There is an outside, however—and it is science.

16. Nadezshda Mandelstam, *Hope Against Hope: A Memoir,* translated by Max Hayward (New York: Atheneum, 1970), 90.

17. Ibid., 22.

18. See ibid., 134.

19. Roland Barthes, "What Is Criticism," in *Critical Essays,* translated by Richard Howard (Evanston: Northwestern University Press, 1972), 260. In citing a passage in Barthes that illuminates a possible motive in ideology critique, I do not mean simply to identify him as an ideology critic. This may be one of the many roles that he performed, for instance, in *Mythologies,* but elsewhere with characteristic unpredictability, he unsettles the ground on which demystification occurs when, for instance, he declares that "one cannot 'demystify' from the outside in the name of ownership, but one must steep oneself in the void one is revealing" (*Critical Essays,* 131). And in an essay, "La Mythologie Aujourd'hui," written fourteen years after *Mythologies,* Barthes gives up the method of demystification

in favor of evaluation. The phrase "bourgeois ideology," Barthes tells us in *Roland Barthes* (1971), has gone sour (*Roland Barthes*, translated by Richard Howard [New York: Hill & Wang, 1977], 166). I have argued elsewhere that even in *Mythologies* there are signs of his later abandonment of Marxism, which inspires demystification. Barthes did not share Marx's belief in a substantial historical truth that underlies the mystifications of ideology. If there is only the void, there may be something to be said for the compensations of illusion. (See the chapter on Roland Barthes in my book *The Skeptic Disposition: Deconstruction, Ideology, and Other Matters*, 2d ed. (Princeton: Princeton University Press, 1991). In poststructuralism generally (the exemplary figures are Barthes, Foucault, and Derrida), there is a bias in favor of surfaces and a mistrust of surface/depth and inside/outside distinctions. On the one hand, Foucault openly sets himself against ideological criticism. On the other, the habit of suspicion and the disposition to decode language in poststructuralism suggests an affinity with ideology critique even in Foucault.

20. Chinua Achebe, *Morning Yet on Creation Day* (New York: Doubleday, 1975), 12.

21. Ibid.

22. Tzvetan Todorov, *Nous et les Autres* (Paris: Editions du Seuil, 1989), 426.

23. Leszek Kolakowski, *Modernity on Endless Trial* (Chicago: University of Chicago Press, 1990), 22.

24. Ibid., 25.

25. Ibid., 22.

26. Aijaz Ahmad, *In Theory: Classes, Nations, Literatures* (London: Verso, 1992), 77.

27. Claude Levi-Strauss, *Race and History* (Paris: UNESCO, 1952), 17.

28. Ernest Gellner in *Rationality*, edited by Bryan R. Wilson (Oxford: Basil Blackwood, 1974), 30.

29. Berlin, *The Crooked Timber of Humanity: Chapters in the History of Ideas* (New York: Knopf, 1990), 10, 11.

30. Bernard Williams, *Ethics and the Limits of Philosophy* (Cambridge: Harvard University Press, 1985), 158.

31. Ibid., 159.

32. Marianna Torgovnik, *Gone Primitive: Savage Intellects, Modern Lives* (Chicago: University of Chicago Press, 1990), 245.

33. Charles O. Taylor, *Multiculturalism and the Politics of Recognition*, with commentary by Amy Gutman, edited by Steven C. Rockefeller, Michael Walzer, and Susan Wolf (Princeton: Princeton University Press, 1992).

34. See Amelie Rorty, "The Hidden Politics of Multiculturalism," *Political Theory* (April 1994): 152–166.

35. Quoted in Finkielkraut, *The Defeat of the Mind*, 68.

36. Diane Ravitch, "Multiculturalism: E Pluribus Plures," in *Debating P.C.: The Controversy Over Political Correctness on College Campuses*, edited by Paul Berman (New York: Dell, 1992), 275–276.

37. Talal Asad, in *Writing Culture: The Poetics and Politics of Ethnography* (Berkeley: University of California Press, 1986), 157–158.

38. Tzvetan Todorov, *The Conquest of America*, translated by Richard Howard (New York: Harper & Row, 1984), 16.

39. Berlin, *The Crooked Timber*, 13.

40. Kolakowski, *Modernity on Endless Trial*, 53.

41. Ibid., 28, 29.

42. Richard Rorty, *Contingency, Irony, and Solidarity* (New York: Cambridge University Press, 1989), 45.

43. Robert D'Amico, *Historicism and Knowledge* (New York: Routledge, 1989), 68.

44. Ibid., 26.

45. The attempt to discredit empiricism as a worthy intellectual activity in favor of a view that says that all "objective" observation is ideologically motivated and therefore distorted can only impoverish a field. What it may do is inhibit the ambition to accumulate facts that contribute to our knowledge of the world. It introduces a self-defeating doubt at every stage of our effort to achieve positive knowledge of things.

46. Mandelstam, *Hope Against Hope*, 114.

47. Milosz, Czeslaw, *The Captive Mind* (New York: Vintage, 1990), 200.

48. Ibid., 211.

49. Julien Benda, *The Betrayal of the Intellectuals*, translated by Richard Aldington (Boston: Beacon Press, 1955), 182.

50. Ibid., 215.

51. Richard Rorty has argued for the importance of enlarging the sense of solidarity in the effort to mitigate "the pain and humiliation of others." But he is steadfastly opposed to the Kantian universalism that affirms a "humanity as such." His antifoundationalism is so strenuous that it at times blurs his admirable moral ambitions.

> Consider . . . the attitude of contemporary American liberals to the unending hopelessness and misery of the lives of the young blacks in American cities. Do we say that these people must be helped because they are our fellow human beings? We may, but it is much more persuasive, morally as well as politi-

cally, to describe them as our fellow Americans—to insist that it is outrageous that an *American* should live without hope. *Contingency, Irony, and Solidarity* (Cambridge: Cambridge University Press, 1989), 191.

But it is outrageous that anyone should live without hope, even illegal aliens. Rorty may be psychologically realistic when he says that our sense of solidarity is strongest when those with whom solidarity is expressed are thought of as " 'one of us' where 'us' means something smaller and more local than the human race." But psychological realism does not adequately explain or justify a philosophical objection to a universal morality that wants to mitigate the pain and cruelty suffered by all human beings.

2. The Postmodern Liberalism of Richard Rorty

1. Bernard Williams, *Moral Luck* (Cambridge: Cambridge University Press, 1981), 76–77.
2. Richard Rorty, *Contingency, Irony, and Solidarity* (Cambridge: Cambridge University Press, 1989), 53.
3. Ibid., 5.
4. Carl Becker, *The Heavenly City of Eighteenth-Century Philosophers* (New Haven: Yale University Press, 1932).
5. Rorty and Harold Bloom, admirers of each other's work, are an odd couple: Bloom all anxiety, Rorty with scarcely a trace of it.
6. Rorty, *Contingency*, 89.
7. Rorty, "Foucault/Dewey/Nietzsche," *Raritan* 9, no. 4 (1990): 2.
8. Rorty, *Contingency*, 102.
9. Ibid., 90.
10. Ibid., 23, 24, 25.
11. Ibid., 90.
12. Rorty, *Consequences of Pragmatism* (Minneapolis: University of Minnesota Press, 1982), 200.
13. John Stuart Mill, *Essays on Politics and Culture*, edited by Gertrude Himmelfarb (Gloucester, Mass.: Peter Smith, 1973), 172.
14. William James, *Pragmatism and Four Essays from the Meaning of Truth* (New York: New American Library, 1974), 197.
15. Ibid., 192–193.
16. Ibid., 62.
17. Rorty, *Contingency, Irony, and Solidarity*, 86.
18. Ibid., 85.
19. Cornel West, *Race Matters* (Boston: Beacon Press, 1993), 14.

20. Ibid., 58.

21. Rorty, *Contingency*, 73.

22. *Critical Inquiry* (Spring, 1990), 638.

23. Rorty, *Consequences*, 172.

24. The odd thing about Rorty's pragmatism is that it is more philosophical (in Rorty's pejorative sense) than pragmatic. In practice, we do not behave toward one another as if we were locked into a perspective; we act as if we can communicate with each other.

25. Rorty, "Postmodernist Bourgeois Liberalism," in *Hermeneutics and Praxis*, edited by Robert Hollinger (South Bend, Ind.: University of Notre Dame Press, 1985), 220.

26. Rorty, *Consequences*, 174. Conversation is a Rortyan term that resembles but differs from communication, a Habermasian term that suggests the possibility of understanding among persons of different perspectives. Conversation is internal to a particular community, communication (potentially at least) universal. In *The Promise of Pragmatism* (Chicago: University of Chicago Press, 1994), John Patrick Diggins conflates conversation and communication in a discussion of the ungrounded character of pragmatism and misses the significant distinction between them. "One philosopher places his hopes in communication, the other in conversation. Confronting the dilemma of modernity, both believe philosophy can talk its way out of the problems it has thought itself into. Can it?" (426).

27. Rorty's antiuniversalism, curiously enough, echoes that of the founder of conservatism, Joseph de Maistre: "There is no such thing as *man* in the world. I have seen, during my life, Frenchmen, Italians, Russians, etc. But as far as *man* is concerned, I declare that I have never in my life met him; if he exists, he is unknown to me." See Stephen Holmes, *The Anatomy of Antiliberalism* (Cambridge: Harvard University Press, 1993), 14.

28. Leszek Kolakowski, *Modernity on Endless Trial* (Chicago: University of Chicago, 1990), 22.

29. Rorty, *Contingency*, 51–52.

30. Rorty, *Consequences*, xlii.

31. Jean Amery, *At the Mind's Limits: Contemplations by a Survivor on Auschwitz and Its Realities* (New York: Schocken Books, 1986), 90–91.

32. Quoted in Finkielkraut, *The Defeat of the Mind* (New York: Columbia University Press, 1995.

33. In a recent book, *Postethnic America* (New York: Basic Books, 1995), David Hollinger formulates an attractive third way that would avoid the pitfalls of particularism and universalism. "Cosmopolitanism promotes multiple identities, emphasizes the dynamic and changing character of many

groups, and is responsive to the potential for creating new cultural combinations"(3). The advantage of cosmopolitanism is that, on the one hand, it respects diversity as universalists tend not to do, and, on the other, it has a "profound suspicion of enclosures," which particularist versions of pluralism promote. Hollinger's view is critical of Rorty's ethnocentrism and compatible with the views of Isaiah Berlin and Bernard Williams, which I have cited. However, I would not want to surrender the universalist idea completely, because, as I have tried to make clear, it is morally necessary to be able to invoke universals in human affairs.

3. Matthew Arnold, Critic of Ideology

1. Fredric Jameson, *Postmodernism; or, The Cultural Logic of Late Capitalism* (Durham: Duke University Press, 1991), 180.

2. John B. Thompson, *Studies in the Theory of Ideology* (Cambridge and New York: Cambridge University Press, 1984), 5.

3. Friedrich Nietzsche, *The Birth of Tragedy and the Genealogy of Morals*, translated by Francis Golffing (Garden City, N.Y.: Doubleday, 1956), 256. William James, *The Will to Believe and Other Essays in Popular Philosophy (1897) Bound with Human Immortality (1898)* (New York: Dover, 1956), 21. See also Mark Jones "Recuperating Arnold: Romanticism and Modern Projects of Disinterestedness," *Boundary*, 2 (Summer 1991): 85.

4. Arnold, *Culture and Anarchy*, edited by J. Dover Wilson (London: Cambridge University Press, 1955–1971), 111.

5. "The Function of Criticism at the Present Time," in *Matthew Arnold: Selected Essays*, chosen and with an introduction by Noel Annan (London: Oxford University Press, 1964), 23–24. David Bromwich notes an anticipation of Arnold's praise of Burke in Hazlitt's assertion that a "test of the sense and candour of anyone belonging to the opposite party [is] whether he allowed Burke to be a great man." "The Genealogy of Disinterestedness," *Raritan* 1 (Spring 1982): 64.

6. Arnold, "The Function of Criticism," 29.

7. *Culture and Anarchy*, 48.

8. Bromwich, "The Genealogy of Disinterestedness," 85.

9. Terry Eagleton, *Ideology: An Introduction* (London: Verso, 1991), 166.

10. Chris Baldick, *The Social Mission of English Criticism, 1848–1932* (New York: Oxford University Press, 1983), 24.

11. Arnold, *Culture and Anarchy*, 109.

12. George Eliot, *Middlemarch* (New York: Penguin Books, 1965), 845–846.

13. Quoted in Vassilis Lambropoulos, *The Rise of Eurocentrism: Anatomy of Interpretation* (Princeton: Princeton University Press, 1993), 119.
14. Ibid., 118.
15. *A Selection from Scrutiny*, 2 vols. (Cambridge: Cambridge University Press, 1968), 1:261.
16. Lionel Trilling, *The Liberal Imagination* (Garden City, N.Y.: Doubleday, 1953), 287.
17. T. S. Eliot, "Arnold and Pater," in *Selected Essays* (New York: Harcourt Brace, 1950), 387.
18. Finkielkraut, *The Defeat of the Mind*, 33.
19. Ibid., 35.
20. Ibid., 38.
21. Patrick McCarthy, *Matthew Arnold and the Three Classes* (New York: Columbia University Press, 1964), 166.
22. Ibid., 152.
23. Arnold, *Culture and Anarchy*, 123.
24. Louis Althusser, *For Marx* (London: Verso, 1990), 80.
25. Edmund Burke, *Reflections on the Revolution in France and the Proceedings in Certain Societies in London Relative to the Event*, edited with an introduction by Thomas H. D. Mahoney (Indianapolis: Bobbs-Merrill, 1955), 98–99.
26. Raymond Williams, *Culture and Society: 1780–1950* [1958], with a new introduction by the author (New York: Columbia University, 1983), 123. Patrick McCarthy cites a letter Arnold wrote that clearly distinguishes him from Burke: "The old order of things had not the virtue which Burke supposed. The Revolution had not the banefulness that he supposed. But neither was the Revolution the commencement, as its friends supposed, of a reign of justice and virtue. It was much rather, as Scherer has called it, 'un dechainement d'instincts confus, un aveugle et immense besoin de renouvellement.' An epoch of concentration and of resistance to the crude and violent people who were imposing their 'renouvellement' on the rest of the world by force was natural and necessary. Burke is to be conceived as the great voice of this epoch. He carried his country with him, and was in some sort a providential person. But he did harm as well as good, for he made concentration too dominant an idea with us, and an idea of which the reign was unduly prolonged. The time for expansion must come, and Burke is of little help to us in presence of such a time. But in his sense of the crudity and tyranny of the French revolutionists, I do not think he was mistaken" (*Matthew Arnold and the Three Classes*, 155–156).
27. Arnold, *Culture and Anarchy*, 127.

28. Wendell Harris makes the case that "in merely criticizing the grounds on which the Liberals were proceeding without offering alternatives, in effect [Arnold] was cutting each issue away from the argument to which his readers were accustomed." ("Interpretive Historicism: 'Signs of the Times' and *Culture and Anarchy* in Their Contexts," in *Nineteenth Century Literature* [March 1990], 455). From this perspective, the criticism that Arnold is a conservative upholding the status quo is misconceived.

29. Arnold, "The Function of Criticism," 23.

30. Zygmunt Bauman, *Modernity and the Holocaust* (New York: Cornell University Press, 1989), 126.

4. The Abandoned Legacy of the New York Intellectuals

1. Richard Hofstadter, *Anti-Intellectualism in American Life* (New York: Knopf, 1963), 394.

2. Terry Cooney, *The Rise of the New York Intellectuals: Partisan Review and Its Circle, 1934–35* (Madison, Wisc.: University of Wisconsin Press, 1986), 256.

3. Clement Greenberg, "Avant-Garde and Kitsch," *Partisan Review* (Fall 1939): 34.

4. Sidney Hook, *Out of Step: An Unquiet Life in the Twentieth Century* (New York: Harper & Row, 1987), 513.

5. Ibid., 514.

6. Ibid., 521.

7. Russell Jacoby, *The Last Intellectuals: American Culture in the Age of Academe* (New York: Basic Books, 1987), 134.

8. See William Phillips, *A Partisan View: Five Decades of the Literary Life* (New York: Stein and Day, 1983), and William Barrett, *The Truants: Adventures Among the Intellectuals* (New York: Doubleday, 1982).

9. Irving Howe, *Politics and the Novel* (New York: Horizon Press, 1957), 20, 22.

10. William Phillips, "What Happened in the 1930's," *Commentary* (September 1962): 212.

11. Cooney, *New York Intellectuals*, 83. See James Farrell, *A Note on Literary Criticism* (New York: Columbia University Press, 1993).

12. Alan Wald, *The New York Intellectuals: The Rise and Decline of the Anti-Stalinist Left from the 1930s to the 1980s* (Chapel Hill: University of North Carolina Press, 1987), 80.

13. It may surprise some readers to see Fiedler in the list of high culturists. His current populism resulted from a conversion experience in the 1960s. Fiedler, the high culturist, is to be found in his first two collections

of essays, *An End to Innocence* (Boston: Beacon Press, 1955) and *No! in Thunder* (Boston: Beacon Press, 1960).

14. See Dwight McDonald, "By Cozzens Possessed," *Commentary* (January 1958): 36–47.

15. Alexander Herzen, *From the Other Shore*, translated by Richard Wollheim (London: Weidenfeld and Nicholson, 1956), 116.

16. *Breakthrough: A Treasury of Contemporary American-Jewish Literature*, edited by Irving Malin and Irwin Stark (Philadelphia: Jewish Publication Society of America, 1964), 2.

17. Ralph Ellison, *Shadow and Act* (New York: 1953, 1964, 1987), 140.

18. See Morris Dickstein, *Double Agent* (New York: Oxford University Press, 1992).

19. Lionel Trilling, "Elements That Are Wanted," *Partisan Review* (September-October 1940): 368.

20. Wald, *Rise and Decline*, 229.

5. Kenneth Burke Revisited

1. Marius Bewley, *The Complex Fate* (London: Chatto and Windus, 1952), 219.

2. Kenneth Burke, *Attitudes Toward History* (Los Altos, Cal.: Hermes, 1959), 331.

3. Bewley, *The Complex Fate*, 223.

4. Ibid., 216–217.

5. Burke, *The Philosophy of Literary Form* (Baton Rouge: Louisiana State University Press, 1941), 302.

6. Burke, *Language as Symbolic Action: Essays on Life, Literature, and Method* (Berkeley: University of California Press, 1966), 16.

7. Burke, *Permanence and Change*, rev. ed. (Berkeley: University of California Press, 1984), 3.

8. Ibid., 6.

9. Burke, *Counter-Statement* (Los Altos, Cal.: Hermes, 1953), xii.

10. Ibid., 106.

11. Burke, *Attitudes Toward History*, 74.

12. Ibid., 180.

13. Burke, *Permanence and Change*, 294.

14. Sidney Hook, "The Technique of Mystification" (review of *Attitudes Toward History*), in *Critical Responses to Kenneth Burke, 1924–1966*, edited by William H. Rueckert (Minneapolis: University of Minnesota Press, 1969), 93. Reprinted from *Partisan Review*, 4 (December 1937): 57–62.

15. Burke, *Language as Symbolic Action*, 52.

16. Burke, *Attitudes Toward History*, 261.

17. Burke, *A Rhetoric of Motives* (New York: Prentice Hall, 1950), 122.

18. Roland Barthes, *Mythologies*, translated by Annette Lavers (New York: Hill & Wang, 1957), 159.

19. Burke, *The Rhetoric of Religion: Studies in Logology* (Boston: Beacon Press, 1961), vi.

20. Burke, *Language as Symbolic Action*, 469–470.

21. See Burke, *A Rhetoric of Motives*, 110.

22. Burke, *The Rhetoric of Religion*, 300.

23. William H. Rueckert, "Burke's Verbal Drama," in Rueckert, ed., *Critical Responses*, 348. Reprinted from *The Nation* (February 1962): 150.

24. Burke, *Towards a Better Life* (New York: Harcourt Brace, 1932), 195.

25. Burke, *A Rhetoric of Motives*, 14–15.

26. John Crowe Ransom, "An Address to Kenneth Burke," in Rueckert, ed., *Critical Responses*, 154. Reprinted from *Kenyon Review*, 4 (Spring 1942): 219–237.

27. Burke, *A Grammar of Motives* (Berkeley: University of California Press, 1969), 451.

28. Ibid., 128.

29. Burke, *Permanence and Change*, 121.

30. Max Black, "A Review of 'A Grammar of Motives,'" in Rueckert, ed., *Critical Responses*, 168. Reprinted from *Philosophical Review*, 55 (July 1946): 487–490.

31. See Giles Gunn, *The Criticism of Culture and the Culture of Criticism* (New York: Oxford University Press, 1987).

32. Bewley, *The Complex Fate*, 216–217.

33. Burke, *Attitudes Toward History*, 311.

34. Ibid., 106.

35. Ibid., 107.

36. Burke, *Language as Symbolic Action*, 305.

37. Frank Lentricchia, *Criticism and Social Change* (Chicago: University of Chicago Press, 1983), 85.

38. Ibid., 20.

6. Ideology and Ethical Criticism

1. Marius Bewley, *The Complex Fate* (London: Chatto and Windus, 1952), 216–217.

2. Wayne Booth, *The Company We Keep: An Ethics of Fiction* (Berkeley: University of California Press, 1988), 3.

3. Henry James, "The Art of Fiction," in *The Art of Criticism*, edited by William Veeder and Susan M. Griffin (Chicago: University of Chicago Press, 1986), 180, 181–82.

4. Henry James, Preface to *Portrait of a Lady* in ibid., 289.

5. Booth, *The Company We Keep*, 440–442.

6. Milan Kundera, *The Unbearable Lightness of Being*, translated by Michael Henry Heim (New York: Harper & Row, 1985), 221.

7. Freud on Trial

1. See Frederick Crews, "The Unknown Freud," *The New York Review of Books* (November 18, 1993): 53–66, and Paul Gray, "The Assault on Freud" *Time* (November 29, 1993): 47–51.

2. In a public exchange I had with Crews, he reproached me for characterizing him as "a resentful renegade" and a "parricide." It is true, of course, as he points out, that I know nothing of his motives. In characterizing him in this fashion, I did not mean to attribute motives. I was responding to the animus of his article and to the impression it created. (See *Dissent* [Fall 1995]: 530–532.) It is strange to me that I have made Crews a target of critique in a book about ideological interpretation, as I not only admire his work as a literary critic but also find his own criticisms of the ideological obsessions in literary studies persuasive. But his recent work on Freud makes him an inevitable target. Crews's attack on Freud brings to mind Tolstoy's diatribe against Shakespeare. Tolstoy characterizes *King Lear* inconsistently as a work without value and as the immoral product of an evil genius. Tolstoy simply could not deny Shakespeare's imaginative power. The venom of his response is in effect a tribute to that power. What holds true for Tolstoy on Shakespeare may hold true for Crews on Freud.

3. Crews, "The Unknown Freud," 56.

4. Ibid.

5. "What Is an Author," in *The Foucault Reader*, edited by Paul Rabinow (New York: Pantheon Books, 1984), 116. It is not altogether clear how Foucault means this characterization as an evaluation of Freud's achievement. Paul Robinson cites Foucault in his defense of Freud as someone who created "an endless possibility of discourse" (*Freud and His Critics* [Berkeley: University of California Press, 1993], 270). But this tells us nothing of the validity of the discourse. In *The History of Sexuality*, Foucault reveals himself a critic of Freud's hypothesis of repression. We should be cautious about reading *The History of Sexuality* back into "What Is an

Author?" for Foucault's judgment of Freud, but I think it fair to say that nowhere in his work does he show himself to be a Freudian. Paul Robinson's recent book, *Freud and His Critics*, for all its appearance of judiciousness, is at bottom the work of an idolater. Somewhat disingenuously Robinson characterizes Frank Sulloway, Jeffrey Masson, and Adolf Grünbaum as Freud's most powerful critics only to demonstrate their failures of understanding and their misguided criticisms. The implication is that all criticisms of Freud are bound to fail. On occasion, Robinson concedes the justice of a criticism of Freud, for instance, that "concepts like resistance, ambivalence, overdetermination and reaction formation let the analyst have it both ways" (208). But the concession stops short of exploring the implications. It is as if Robinson wants to disarm Freud's critics by anticipating the criticism and formulating it in a manner least damaging to Freud.

6. Sigmund Freud, *The Interpretation of Dreams*, in *The Basic Writings of Sigmund Freud*, edited by A. A. Brill (New York: Modern Library, 1938), 308.

7. See Peter Brooks, *Reading for the Plot* (Cambridge: Harvard University Press, 1984).

8. Sigmund Freud, *Three Case Histories: "The Wolf Man," "The Rat Man," and "The Psychotic Doctor Schreber"* (New York: Collier Books, 1963), 112.

9. Ibid., 154.

10. Freud, *Dora: An Analysis of a Case of Hysteria* (New York: Collier Books, 1969), 76.

11. "According to psychoanalytical theory, I told him, every fear corresponded to a former wish which was now repressed; we were therefore obliged to believe the exact opposite of what he had asserted" (Freud, *Three Case Histories*, 24). The view that consciousness is a negation of the unconscious presumes the homogeneity of consciousness and the opposing homogeneity of unconsciousness. But there is abundant evidence of ambivalence and contradiction within both consciousness and the unconscious to cast doubt upon the accuracy of this bipolar model of the self.

12. Freud, *Three Case Histories*, 167.

13. Jacques Bouveresse, *Wittgenstein Reads Freud: The Myth of the Unconscious*, translated by Carol Cosman (Princeton: Princeton University Press, 1995), 100.

14. Ibid., 123.

15. Robinson, *Freud and His Critics*, 117.

16. Harold Rosenberg, *Act and Actor* (Chicago: University of Chicago Press, 1970), 16.

17. Freud, *Three Case Histories*, 19.

18. Sigmund Freud, *Standard Edition of the Complete Psychological Works* (24 vols.), edited and translated by James Strachey (London: Norton, 1953–1994), 13:233.

8. The Passion of Reason

1. Saul Bellow, *To Jerusalem and Back* (New York: Viking Press, 1979), 58.

2. George Steiner, *Language and Silence: Essays on Language, Literature, and the Inhuman* (New York: Atheneum, 1967), 168.

3. Primo Levi, *The Drowned and the Saved*, translated by Raymond Rosenthal (New York: Vintage Books, 1989), 142.

4. Jean Amery, *At the Mind's Limits: Contemplations by a Survivor on Auschwitz and Its Realities*, translated by Sidney Rosenfeld and Stella P. Rosenfeld, foreword by Alexander Stille (New York: Schocken Books, 1986), 3–4.

5. Ibid., 11.

6. Levi, *The Drowned and the Saved*, 145.

7. Ibid.

8. Amery, *At the Mind's Limits*, 14.

9. Ibid., 90–91.

10. Levi, *The Drowned and the Saved*, 136.

11. Jean Amery, *Radical Humanism*, edited and translated by Sidney Rosenfeld and Stella P. Rosenfeld (Bloomington: Indiana University Press, 1984), 136. Like Amery, Nadezhda Mandelstam is witness to personal ineffectuality in the presence of the pervasive terror of the state. She speaks of Soviet terror as having "totally exposed—not in theory but in practice—all the assumptions on which our humanism rested" (*Hope Against Hope: A Memoir* [New York: Atheneum, 1970], 322). Like Amery, Mandelstam views the abandonment of humanism to the nihilist view that "everything is permitted" as calamitous (325). But unlike Amery, Mandelstam is not a rationalist. She tends to identify rationalism with the nihilistic utilitarianism Dostoevsky excoriated in his novels. She has recourse not to reason but to poetry, which functions for her as a religious faith:

> Poetry does indeed have a very special place in this country. It arouses people and shapes their minds. No wonder the birth of our new intelligentsia is accompanied by a craving for poetry never seen before—it is the golden treasury in which our values are preserved; it brings people back to life, awakens their conscience and stirs them to thought. (333)

Needless to say, this recourse did not exist for Amery.

12. Zygmunt Bauman, *Modernity and the Holocaust* (New York: Cornell University Press, 1989), 5.

13. Cited in ibid., 25.

Hannah Arendt, *Eichmann in Jerusalem: A Report on the Banality of Evil* (New York: Viking Press, 1964), 108.

14. Quoted in Albert Camus, *The Rebel* (Harmondsworth, Middlesex: Penguin Books, 1965), 15.

15. Amery, *At the Mind's Limits*, 67.

16. See Terrence Des Pres, *The Survivor* (New York: Oxford University Press, 1966), 97.

17. Levi, *The Drowned and the Saved*, 69.

18. Ibid., 139–140.

19. Primo Levi, *Survival at Auschwitz: The Nazi Assault on Humanity*, translated by Stuart Woolf (New York: Macmillan, 1976), 102.

20. Levi, *The Drowned and the Saved*, 60.

21. Ibid., 24.

22. See Tzvetan Todorov, *Face à l'extrême* (Paris: Editions du Seuil, 1991), 294–297.

23. Levi, *The Drowned and the Saved*, 148.

24. Cynthia Ozick, *Metaphor and Memory* (New York: Knopf, 1989), 47.

25. Levi, *Survival at Auschwitz*, 79.

26. Ibid., 111.

27. Levi, *The Drowned and the Saved*, 147.

Concluding Remarks

1. George Levine, Peter Brooks, Jonathan Culler, Marjorie Garber, E. Ann Kaplan, and Catherine R. Stimpson,"Speaking for the Humanities," American Council of Learned Societies, ACLS Occasional Paper, no. 7 (1989): 11. The title of the manifesto is revealing. The authors appear to assume in their quarrel with their adversaries (Allan Bloom, Lynne Cheney, and William Bennett) that the humanities is what they say they are and that the critics are adversaries of the humanities. One does not have to agree with Bloom, Cheney, and Bennett to see that the issue constitutes a quarrel about the condition of the humanities, in which both sides have a stake. The title in effect takes possession of the humanities and makes it seem as if a quarrel with the view set forth by its authors is a quarrel with the humanities per se, and not with a specific conception of it.

2. Ibid., 10.

Index

Achebe, Chinua, 10, 21
Adorno, Theodore, 152
Aesthetic criticism, 12
Aesthetic value, 1, 6, 11
Affective fallacy, 5
Ahmad, Aijaz, 23
Althusser, Louis, 3, 75, 95, 181n15
Amery, Jean: on auto-destruction of intellectual in concentration camps, 154–55; on dignity, 156–57; on Enlightenment universalism, 157, 174; on faith, 153, 155–56; on reason, 158; on resentment, 159–62; on suicide, 157, 162, 168; on tor-
ture, 162; on uselessness of culture in camps, 163–64
Arendt, Hannah, 152, 158
Arnold, Matthew: on "aliens" as spiritual elite, 69, 71, 72, 73, 74; antirevolutionary views of, 68–69; on "[Edmund] Burke's return upon himself," 65, 66, 77–78, 79; on class, 64, 67–68, 73–74; on disinterestedness and objectivity, 62–64, 65–67, 79; on disinterestedness, truth, and justice, 80–81; on "force until right is ready," 68–69; on free play of thought, 78; on French

Greenberg, Clement, 85, 87, 91
Grünbaum, Adolf, 129, 142, 143, 144,
  145, 150, 191*n*5
Guess, Raymond, 179*n*7
Gunn, Giles, 111

Habermas, Jürgen, 51, 129, 145
Harris, Wendell, 187*n*28
Heart of Darkness, 6, 10–11
Hebraism in Arnold, 65, 70
Hegelianism, 75
Hemingway, Ernest: Ellison on, 93–94
Hermeneutics: science and, 142–45; of
  suspicion, 2, 3, 18
Herzen, Alexander, 91
Heuristics, 133
Historicism: compared with history,
  37–38; as theology of historical
  necessity, 37, 38–39
Hitler, Adolph, 104
Hofstadter, Richard on *Partisan Review*,
  82
Hollinger, David, 185*n*33
Holocaust: as demystifier of "human-
  ity," 151, 170, 171; as essence of
  Nazism, 24; fate of believers versus
  agnostics in, 155; moral life in, 167;
  revisionism, 5, 152; as shrouded
  with taboos, 152; trivialization of,
  152; suicide and, 162–63; survivors'
  guilt and, 162–63, 169; totalitarian-
  ism in, 154–55, 157; *see also* Amery,
  Jean; Levi, Primo
Hook, Sidney, 86, 87, 104
Howe, Irving, 88–89
Huckleberry Finn, 116, 117, 122, 125
Humor, ethical use of, 121–22

Ideology: as concept of recent invention, 17; as contaminator of art, 97;
  as culture, 13–15; as descriptive,
  positive, and pejorative, 179*n*7; distinguished from false consciousness, 3; as domination, 2, 6; as false
  consciousness, 2, 3–4; historical

vicissitudes of, 180*n*11; Howe's view
  of, in political novels, 89; the limits
  of, 127; as neither true nor false, 3,
  4; as omnipresent, 19, 172–73; versus ethics, 118; versus scientific
  knowledge, 3
Ideology critique: aesthetic texts and,
  9–12; of class, race, and gender
  interests in cultural expressions, 15;
  compared with cultural criticism, 12;
  cultural studies and, 174; as desire
  for truth and justice, 17; as dogmatic, 24; Enlightenment and, 18; as
  ethical discourse, 16; as ideology,
  18–19; master texts of, 78–79; objectivity and partiality in, 16–17; as part
  of radicalization of literary academy,
  87; as representing constituencies of
  dispossessed, 42; as search for
  underlying motives, 180*n*14; as
  unmasking false consciousness and
  untruth, 2–3; as violator of texts, 20
Imperialism, 4, 5; modern novel and,
  6–7; *see also* Colonialism
Impersonality, 71
India, 23–24
Intentional fallacy, 5
Intolerance: of differences, 4–5; ethnocentrism as, 25; of religious and
  metaphysical views in, 47–48; *see
  also* Differences; Discrimination;
  Racism
Irony of Rorty, 48, 54, 59

Jacoby, Russell, 87, 88
James, Henry, 116–17
Jameson, Fredric, 18–19, 74, 180*n*14,
  181*n*15
James, William, 52–53, 63
Joubert, Joseph, 68
Joyce, James, 7, 71

Keats, John, 110
Kolakowski, Leszek, 22–23, 25, 33,
  34–36, 42, 58, 174, 175